MAD:

What the World Needs Now Is a Little Madness

By

Mark Falzon

Copyright © 2025 by MAD Ventures Australia Pty Ltd
ABN: 86 623 423 558 and Mark Falzon

Self published in Australia by:
MAD Ventures Australia Pty Ltd
www.mad.vc

All rights reserved.

No part of this book may be reproduced by any mechanical, photographic or electronic process, nor may it be stored in a retrieval system, transmitted, or otherwise copied for public or private use, other than for "fair use" in brief quotations embodied in articles and reviews, without prior written permission of the publisher.

The author provides the information in this book for educational purposes only. Nothing contained herein should be taken as personal or professional advice.

Readers should seek financial, legal and other professional guidance appropriate to their circumstances and to the jurisdiction in which they operate.

The intent of the author is to offer insight into the systems, structures and inner capacities required to design a more coherent, regenerative and purpose-driven world. This book explores the redeployment of capital, the evolution of leadership, the architecture of integrated investing and the pathways toward building ventures, communities and movements that make a difference.

By choosing to apply any ideas from this book, the reader accepts full responsibility for their own actions and outcomes.

MAD - What the World Needs Now Is a Little Madness
/ Mark Falzon

ISBN: 978-0-6457675-3-7
eBook ISBN: 978-0-6457675-2-0

FOREWORD

by Mac Christopherson

For more than ten years, Mark and I have worked side by side, building a partnership grounded in deep respect, openness, and a genuine care for each other's growth. That foundation is why MAD exists, and why this book exists. When two people can challenge each other, stretch each other, and stay completely aligned in purpose, the work becomes stronger and more meaningful.

Anyone who knows Mark will recognise his presence in every chapter. He has a way of seeing people clearly and seeing the real problem with equal precision, and he does it with a visionary sense of what is possible beyond the moment in front of him and in front of the world. That is why founders, investors, and leaders trust him. Mark does not just advise; he elevates.

One of the things I value most about him is how quickly he brings clarity. When I am facing a big problem, I can call Mark, talk for three minutes, and walk away grounded and clear. That blend of precision, empathy, and directness is Mark's real genius, and it is threaded through every page of this book.

The ideas in this book reflect the spirit of what we have built at MAD. Our shared philosophy is simple: real change happens when grounded people take on hard, meaningful problems with courage, integrity, and a willingness to go deeper than the market usually asks of them. Mark has taken that worldview and shaped it into a narrative that invites readers into the same clarity we aim to bring to the founders and systems we support.

This book matters now because the world does not need more noise; it needs people who are willing to step into purpose and meaningful work. That sits at the heart of everything I care about, and it sits at the heart of this book too.

I admire how Mark has given voice to ideas we have shaped together over a decade. It reflects the clarity and depth he brings to this work, and why our partnership continues to be such a strong foundation for MAD.

If this book resonates with you, I hope it sparks something: a decision, a shift, or a question you have been avoiding. Because, as we have learned through building MAD, meaningful progress rarely starts with certainty. It starts with someone willing to take the next step, even when the ground is not fully mapped.

Enjoy the journey.
Mac

AUTHOR'S NOTE

This book began as a question.

A simple question, but one that refused to let go.

What kind of world could we build if capital behaved as if the future mattered?

For more than forty years, I have lived inside companies as a founder, operator, builder and mentor. I have witnessed the courage of entrepreneurs who create something from nothing, the exhaustion of leaders asked to carry more than they should, the distortions caused by misaligned capital, and the quiet brilliance of people who want to make a difference but lack the structures to do so.

Again and again, I saw the same pattern.

The ventures that could have changed the world failed for reasons that had nothing to do with capability or technology. They failed because the system around them was not designed to support coherence. They failed because capital, the bloodstream of civilisation, was out of alignment with the work the world most needed.

MAD was born from that frustration, and from a deeper belief that the world does not lack talent or innovation or imagination. It lacks a philosophy of capital that honours the interconnected nature of life, purpose, community, systems and meaning.

This book is not a manual for investing, nor a manifesto for reform. It is an invitation, a bridge between what is and what is possible. It is the story of how we can redesign the tools that shape our world, and how we can rise to meet the challenges of our time with courage, coherence and a little madness.

Because what the world needs now is not more caution.

It needs more courage.

Not more fragmentation, but more integration.

Not more spectators, but more stewards.

This book is my contribution to that work.

Thank you for reading it, and for the difference you are making.

Mark Falzon
New South Wales, Australia

INTRODUCTION

How to Read This Book

This book asks you to imagine something bold, then grounds that imagination in the practical architecture of how to build it.

You will move through three distinct arcs:

Part I, The Descent

We begin in possibility, then dive into the realities of the world as it is. Environmental instability, political fragmentation, social disconnection and the collapse of meaning. This descent is not meant to discourage you, but to clarify the stakes.

Part II, The Bridge

Here we move from diagnosis to design. You will discover the Venture Compass, the Gap, the X Factor, and the integrated worldview that binds meaning, markets, culture and capital into one coherent whole. You will meet the architecture of capital that MAD created, and understand why structure is moral design.

Part III, The Return

We rise again into vision, but now it is earned. You will see the Possible Planet through a new lens, and understand how founders, investors, communities and movements can build it. The journey ends with an invitation, not a conclusion.

How to use this book

You do not need to be an investor to understand the language of systems, coherence or regeneration. You do not need to be a founder to appreciate the pressures and possibilities of building something meaningful. You may be a policymaker, a student, a philanthropist, a business leader, a member of a family office, or simply someone who cares about the future.

Wherever you sit in the system, this book offers three things:

1. **Clarity**, a way of seeing the world as a set of interconnected forces.
2. **Courage**, a reminder that the future belongs to those willing to imagine boldly.
3. **Capability**, a framework for designing systems that heal rather than harm.

This book is written to be read linearly, but you may also return to chapters as tools. The Compass, the architecture of capital, the principles of integration and the reflections on leadership are designed to stand alone as much as they work together.

Read this book with an open mind and a steady heart.

We are living through the most important transition in human history.

How we allocate capital, how we support founders, and how we design systems will shape the next century.

This book is one way to begin that work.

ACKNOWLEDGEMENTS

This book would not exist without the people who walked beside me, challenged me, inspired me and helped me see the world more clearly.

To Mac Christopherson
There are partnerships that sit on the surface of work, and there are those that sit at the centre of a life. Mac has been the latter for me. Over the last decade, he has been a partner, a challenger, a stabilising force, and a creative ally in the truest sense of the word. MAD was not built by one person. It was built in the space between two people who chose to hold themselves to a higher standard, to stay honest, to stay open, and to stay committed to something larger than either of us individually.

Mac has brought clarity when complexity was at its peak, steadiness when the ground was shifting, and a fierce commitment to integrity that has shaped not just our work, but the philosophy behind it. His ability to see through noise, to ask the right question at the right moment, and to hold the line on what matters has strengthened every chapter of this book and every chapter of MAD.

More than that, he has been a mirror. He has held up the places I could grow, the ideas that needed to sharpen, the opportunities that needed to be taken, and he has done it with respect, care, and an unwavering belief in what we are building together. This book carries his fingerprints in ways most readers will never see, and that is exactly why I want to acknowledge it here.

MAD exists because of our partnership. The ideas in these pages exist because of the years we have spent refining, debating, distilling, and elevating the worldview behind them. I am grateful for his trust, his intelligence, his loyalty, and the friendship that has grown alongside the work.

Thank you, Mac, for the decade you have invested, the clarity you have brought, and the depth you bring to everything we build together.

To our **Board and the MAD Ambassadors**, whose collective wisdom, lived experience and heart form the village behind this movement. You are the proof that community multiplies what capital alone cannot.

To the **founders** who trusted us with your dreams, your fears, your hopes and your missions, you taught me more about courage than any textbook ever could. This book is dedicated to you and to the difference you make every day.

To the **investors, family offices** and **philanthropic partners** who saw the potential of integrated capital long before it was fashionable, thank you for your belief and your stewardship.

To my **family - Michelle, Ruby and Jesse**, whose love is my anchor and whose encouragement gave me the space to think, reflect and write. Every chapter of this book carries your imprint.

And finally, to everyone who feels the pull to make a difference, this book is for you.

Your courage is the quiet force that will shape the century.

TABLE OF CONTENTS

Foreword i
Author's Note iv
Introduction vii
Acknowledgements x

Prologue: The Possible Planet - The Sanity of Madness 1
Part I: The Descent 9
Chapter 1: The Capital Paradox 11
Chapter 2: Systems in Collapse 20
Chapter 3: The Crisis of Meaning 31
Chapter 4: When Growth Stopped Meaning Progress 43
Chapter 5: The Origin of MAD 57

Part II: The Bridge 71
Chapter 6: The Venture Compass 73
Chapter 7: Integration Beyond Impact 90
Chapter 8: The Architecture of MAD Capital 107
Chapter 9: Engineering Repeatable Outcomes 120
Chapter 10: The Multipliers 136
Chapter 11: The Movement of MAD 153
Chapter 12: Capital of the Heart 167

Chapter 13: The Possible Planet... 186

Part III: The Return..201
Chapter 14: The Beautiful Madness of Belief........................203

The Beautiful Madness of Belief..218
Epilogue: Proof in Practice..220
About the Author 223

PROLOGUE
THE POSSIBLE PLANET
- THE SANITY OF MADNESS

The Possible Planet

We stand at the threshold of a remarkable possibility. For the first time in human history, we possess the tools, knowledge, wealth, and networks to build a world that works for everyone, everywhere, within the boundaries of the living planet that sustains us.

Imagine this world.

Energy is abundant and clean, drawn from sunlight, wind, heat beneath our feet, and the rhythms of tides. Cities shimmer with quiet movement, transport electric and fluid, air clear enough that the horizon feels closer. Oceans teem again with life, their surfaces dotted not by oil slicks but by regenerative farms cultivating carbon-absorbing kelp. Fields are alive with microbes and pollinators, soil breathing back its lost fertility. Food is local and global at once, grown through vertical gardens and precision fermentation, traded across regions not in desperation but in reciprocity.

Health systems no longer chase illness; they sustain vitality. Every child is born into a world where nutrition, clean water, and healthcare are basic infrastructure, not privileges of geography. Longevity is not measured by years alone but by quality of life, mental clarity, connection, belonging. Education flows freely through the networked mind of the planet. An eight-year-old in Nairobi or Nanjing can access the same immersive learning as one in New York, AI tutors that teach empathy as well as algebra, languages as well as listening.

Work has evolved from extraction to creation. Technology, once feared as the enemy of labour, now augments human creativity. Machines perform repetition; people perform imagination. The line between craft and science has blurred: farmers are data scientists, and data scientists design ecosystems. Businesses are not engines of accumulation but instruments of purpose. Value is measured not only by profit but by contribution, how an enterprise enriches the web of life it inhabits.

Communities thrive in resilience. Time itself feels slower, more deliberate. The weekend returns. Art, play, and conversation are no longer luxuries; they are expressions of a civilisation secure enough to explore its own depth. And under all of this hums a quiet harmony, the sense that humanity has finally remembered what it is here to do: to make life more alive.

This vision is not utopian fantasy. It is already latent in the world we live in. The technologies exist. The capital exists. The knowledge exists. The will flickers everywhere, in founders designing circular economies, in investors questioning old assumptions, in policy architects re-imagining the role of government not as controller but as catalyst. The possible planet is not beyond reach. It is only beyond our current imagination of what money and power are for.

The Dragon We Face

And yet, this is not the world we have built.

Our atmosphere thickens each year with the exhaust of progress. The great oceans that once gave us life now choke on our debris. Scientists find microplastics in the bloodstreams of newborns, carbon in the ice of ancient glaciers, mercury in the muscles of fish that sustain coastal communities. Soil, the skin of the earth, erodes faster than it regenerates. Forty per cent of arable land is now degraded, and the fertilizers we depend on are made from finite minerals mined at growing cost to ecosystems and people alike.

The political systems meant to guide us have grown brittle. Democracies fragment under the weight of mistrust; authoritarians rise on the promise of simplicity. The information commons that once connected us now divides us, feeding outrage algorithms rather than understanding. Education lags behind reality. We still train young people for industries that no longer exist, using tools older than the Internet itself.

Global health, despite extraordinary advances, shows paradoxical decline. Lifestyle diseases now outpace infectious ones; mental illness shadows prosperity. In the developed world, abundance breeds anxiety; in the developing world, scarcity still kills quietly.

And through it all flows a deeper malaise: a crisis of meaning. We have mastered efficiency but lost coherence. We produce more, communicate faster, live longer, and yet feel increasingly disconnected from one another and from the living systems that sustain us.

At the heart of this fragmentation lies capital. Never has so much wealth been created, and never has so much of it sat idle or misdirected. Over four hundred trillion dollars circulate through global markets; yet the United Nations estimates a four-and-a-half-trillion annual shortfall to achieve even the baseline Sustainable Development Goals. Philanthropic foundations hold endowments measured in trillions, disbursing a fraction each year while crises compound. Venture funds chase unicorn valuations detached from reality; pension funds seek stability in the very industries accelerating collapse.

It is a paradox bordering on tragedy: the power to transform the planet is trapped inside the very system that built the problem.

We are, in mythic terms, a civilisation facing its dragon. The dragon's scales are fear, habit, and short-term reward. It guards a treasure not of gold but of possibility, the capital, imagination, and collaboration that could heal the world if only we dared to claim them.

The Choice - The Bridge We Must Build

Every great story turns on a choice, and ours is no different. We can continue along the path of incremental decline, rational, respectable, suicidal. Or we can choose the sane madness of transformation.

The difference between fantasy and future is design. We do not need more slogans about impact; we need integrated systems that align profit with planetary well-being. The next economy will not be powered by ideology but by integration, by recognising that financial, natural, social, cultural, and intellectual capitals are not competing accounts but dimensions of the same balance sheet.

This is the work of integrated investing: to bring coherence back to capital. To measure not only returns but regeneration. To invest in ventures whose growth strengthens the systems that sustain life. To structure funds that reward patience over speculation, stewardship over extraction. To see every dollar not as a vote for wealth or poverty, but as a design decision in the architecture of civilisation.

At MAD Ventures, we began this work not from abstraction but from necessity. We were operators before we were investors. We saw how good founders suffocate for lack of the right kind of capital, capital that understands timing, context, and purpose. We built our frameworks, our funds, and our philosophy to answer a single question: how can money move through the world as if it belonged to the world?

Our answer is practical and measurable:

- design capital stacks that blend philanthropy's courage with venture's discipline;
- create diagnostic tools, the Venture Compass, to ensure growth is integral, not parasitic;
- measure success through the Integrated Impact Model, where financial outcomes and planetary boundaries share the same dashboard.

But beneath these systems lies something simpler: faith in humanity's capacity to evolve. We are not optimists; we are engineers of possibility.

The Invitation - The Sanity of Madness

So this is the invitation: to become, at last, a mature species, one that treats wealth not as status but as stewardship.

We already know how to cure most diseases, restore forests, clean rivers, and feed billions. We already know how to generate unlimited renewable energy and educate a child anywhere on Earth. What we lack is not technology or capital but conviction, a collective willingness to act as if the future mattered as much as the present quarter.

It will require courage to invest differently, to govern differently, to measure success differently. It will require, in the language of myth, a little madness, the willingness to step beyond the known and build a bridge to the possible.

This book is that bridge. It tells the story of how capital can be re-imagined as a regenerative force; how entrepreneurs, investors, and institutions can align their work with the deepest logic of life itself; and how we, together, can claim the treasure our dragon guards.

The path ahead is neither easy nor certain. But then, it never is in the stories worth telling.

And if we take it, if we dare to design the world our children already dream of, we may yet look back and call this moment what it truly was: **the sanity of madness.**

PART I
THE DESCENT

CHAPTER 1
THE CAPITAL PARADOX

Why Abundance Isn't Alignment

Re-Entering Reality

If the Possible Planet already exists within reach, why haven't we built it?

We are not short of money, intelligence, or technology. The global economy hums with unprecedented liquidity: more than four hundred trillion US dollars in financial assets circulate daily through the bloodstream of markets. Venture funds, sovereign funds, foundations, endowments, and pension schemes overflow with capital. Yet the United Nations estimates a 4.5-trillion-dollar annual shortfall to meet the Sustainable Development Goals, the basic housekeeping list for a liveable planet.

This is the **capital paradox**. Never in human history has so much wealth existed, and never has it been so poorly matched to humanity's needs.

The contradiction is not only moral; it is mechanical. Our financial machinery was built for an age of scarcity and extraction. It cannot yet compute regeneration. The software of capitalism, our incentive structures, risk models, and definitions of fiduciary duty, still rewards short-term optimisation over long-term coherence. The result is an economy in which money multiplies faster than meaning.

The Numbers Behind the Paradox

A few snapshots expose the scale of misalignment:

- **$400 trillion USD** - total global financial assets (Bank for International Settlements, 2025).
- **$4.5 trillion USD** - annual SDG funding gap (UN DP, 2025).
- **5 %** -average yearly payout from philanthropic foundations; the other 95 % typically invested conventionally, often in the very sectors their grants attempt to repair.

- **70 %** -share of global impact-labelled funds that merely rebadge traditional ESG screens, delivering little measurable systems change (GIIN, 2024).
- **< 40 % DPI** -the cash-on-cash return ratio across large venture portfolios; the rest remains paper value (PitchBook, 2024).

The picture is consistent: capital is abundant but inert. It accumulates in pools rather than circulating through the arteries of the real economy.

Large funds, optimised for management fees and scale, now resemble oil tankers, impressive, slow to steer, and prone to inertia. Their size invites risk aversion; their governance demands conformity. The very scale that once promised efficiency has become a drag coefficient.

By contrast, the ventures capable of addressing climate, food, and health crises are often early-scale companies needing **$5 to 15 million**, too large for grants, too small for private-equity mandates. This *missing middle* is where innovation starves. The funds exist; the flow does not.

How the System Misfires
1. Incentive Design

Fund managers are paid to raise, not necessarily to deploy. Two percent of a billion-dollar fund yields twenty million USD a year in management fees, enough to dull the urgency of experimentation. Performance fees depend on exit valuations, so portfolio companies are pressured toward growth at any cost. When the fee structure rewards accumulation over circulation, capital hoards rather than heals.

2. Silos and Fragmentation
Philanthropy, venture, and government operate as separate planets with incompatible atmospheres. Each measures success in its own currency, charitable impact, IRR, electoral cycles, so cooperative oxygen is scarce. The tragedy is that their missions overlap; the architectures do not.

3. Regulatory Myopia
"Fiduciary duty," conceived in the industrial age, still means "maximise short-term financial return." Yet evidence from the past decade shows that environmental and social instability are now the largest financial risks of all. To ignore them is not prudence; it is negligence disguised as tradition.

4. Psychology and Prestige
Behind the spreadsheets lives the oldest human algorithm, fear. Fear of being first, of being wrong, of being seen as

naïve. Capital markets pride themselves on rationality, but money moves through emotion as much as maths. The need to appear sophisticated often overrides the need to be effective.

A Moment in the Field

I remember sitting in a meeting in Sydney a few years ago with a fund administrator whose clients included several large family offices. We had outlined a renewable-energy platform with proven technology and early revenue. The model delivered predictable yield, job creation, and measurable carbon abatement. The manager listened carefully, then asked a single question:
"Who else is in?"

Not *what* the project would achieve, or *how* it reduced risk, but whether the herd had already moved. In that moment I understood that capital follows comfort more than logic. The first investor to move toward the future must always be a little MAD.

The Opportunity Hiding in Plain Sight

If misalignment is our pathology, the cure is astonishingly near. Consider this: reallocating just 1 % of global financial assets each year toward regenerative sectors would release

$4 trillion USD, enough to close the SDG gap within a decade.

The *missing middle*, ventures between seed and IPO, represents both the highest social leverage and the most glaring funding vacuum. These companies already generate revenue; they need growth capital structured for partnership rather than predation.

Family offices and mission-driven institutions are uniquely positioned here. Their time horizons are generational; their governance flexible; their motivation often values-based. When equipped with the right frameworks, like integrated investing, they can act as civilisation's venture catalysts, converting patient wealth into planetary dividends.

A Question of Design

Why does design matter more than intention? Because structure governs behaviour. The architecture of a fund dictates its ethics. If the instruments reward extraction, even noble investors end up extracting. If they reward regeneration, markets will regenerate by reflex.

This is where the next chapters of this book will lead: into the engineering of capital that aligns purpose with performance. But before we design, we must recognise that the problem is not greed; it is geometry.

Our economy is a circle drawn as a line, inputs become outputs, waste becomes externality, and the loop never closes. Integrated investing redraws the shape: money enters, creates value, regenerates the resource base, and returns stronger.

The Seeds of Change

Change is already stirring. Governments are experimenting with blended-finance vehicles, Australia's CEFC, the EU's InvestEU, the US IRA. Foundations are shifting portions of their endowments to mission-aligned portfolios. New instruments, revenue-based finance, green bonds, catalytic tranches, are bridging old divides between philanthropy and profit.

These are early signals of the system remembering what it is for. The 21st century investor is no longer simply allocating assets; they are allocating agency. Each decision either accelerates entropy or designs coherence.

The Choice Ahead

The paradox leaves us with a binary decision. We can treat the Possible Planet as a dream too expensive to pursue, or we can accept that the resources to build it already sit in our accounts. The question is not whether we can afford transformation, but whether we can afford *not* to redesign the machinery of wealth itself.

Because if design created the problem, only design will solve it.

And that work begins with the courage to look at money, not as a static store of value, but as the most powerful story humanity ever wrote. A story we are free to rewrite.

CHAPTER 2
SYSTEMS IN COLLAPSE

The World Between Orders

A Civilisation Out of Rhythm

If capital is the bloodstream of our global economy, then the organs it feeds are our political, ecological, social, and cultural systems. And today, many of those organs are failing at the same time. What we face is not a single crisis but the overlapping of many, climate instability, political fragmentation, cultural disorientation, technological acceleration, and social exhaustion. Each amplifies the others.

We live in what scientists call a "polycrisis." Not separate problems, but connected patterns, feedback loops that reinforce instability.

This is important:
Our challenges are systemic. That means the solutions must be systemic too.

And no system changes without a redesign of capital.

Democracy Under Strain

Across the world, democratic institutions are fraying.
Trust in government is at its lowest point in recorded history. Citizens feel unheard, politicians feel trapped by polarisation, and media ecosystems reward outrage rather than understanding.

According to the Economist Intelligence Unit's Democracy Index, fewer than 20% of the world's population now lives in a "full democracy," down sharply from a decade ago.
The reasons are complex but interconnected:

- rising inequality fractures social cohesion;
- misinformation corrodes shared reality;
- institutional gridlock breeds cynicism;
- globalisation dissolves local belonging without offering a new narrative in return.

The result is a kind of governance paralysis. And while politics stalls, crisis doesn't.

The Environmental Unravelling

The planet is sending signals harder and harder to ignore.

Carbon concentration is now higher than at any point in 800,000 years. Oceans absorb a quarter of all greenhouse gases, becoming more acidic as they do. Coral reefs, nurseries for 25% of marine life, face mass bleaching events. Microplastics have been found in human blood, lung tissue, and even the placentas of newborn children.

Soil degradation affects more than 40% of arable land globally. This is not simply an agricultural issue; it's a civilisation one. Soil is where food, water, and carbon cycles meet. When it collapses, everything collapses.

These issues are not isolated failures. They are symptoms of a system designed for extraction, not regeneration.
A system where GDP measures throughput but not well-being.
A system in which waste is cheap, damage is externalised, and nature has no balance sheet.

As long as capital flows toward extraction and short-term returns, the planet will continue to reflect those incentives.

The Health Paradox

Just as with capital, modern health presents a paradox:
We have more medical knowledge, drugs, devices, and

technology than ever before, yet population-level health outcomes are stagnating or declining.

Chronic lifestyle diseases are now the leading cause of death globally. Mental health disorders account for one of the largest and fastest-growing burdens of disease. Loneliness has been classified by many health systems as an epidemic in its own right.

And while affluent nations struggle with overconsumption, developing nations face undernutrition, unsafe drinking water, and inadequate healthcare infrastructure.

The global health system is a mirror of our capital system: abundance without alignment, technology without integration.

Education Falling Behind the Future

Education, the engine of human advancement, is struggling to keep up with the world it is meant to prepare us for.

The pace of technological change means the skills required today will be different tomorrow. AI capability doubles in power every 9–12 months; education systems take years just to change a curriculum. Workers are thrown into a labour market reshaped by automation, without the tools to adapt.

Young people enter adulthood burdened by debt and uncertainty, unsure how to navigate a world where the only constant is change.

But the deeper issue is cultural:
Education is still structured for an industrial age that no longer exists.
It teaches compliance more than curiosity, memorisation more than adaptability, and competition more than collaboration.
If the learning scaffolds of society don't evolve, neither will the society.

Social Disconnection and the Meaning Crisis

Beyond the visible crises, politics, environment, health, education, lies a subtler one: the collapse of meaning.

People feel more connected digitally than ever, yet more isolated emotionally. Families live closer but speak less. Communities gather less often. Shared rituals have eroded. Belief systems have fragmented. The centre has not held.

This is not philosophical indulgence; it is structural. Societies without shared narratives struggle to coordinate action, especially action as large as rethinking the economy.

This "meaning crisis" has direct economic consequences:

- burnout reduces productivity;
- mistrust reduces civic cooperation;
- anxiety affects consumption and investment patterns;
- fragmented narratives weaken political capacity.

When a civilisation forgets why it exists, it forgets how to build.

Technology: Acceleration Without Direction

AI, robotics, genomics, quantum computing, these tools could be the greatest enablers of human flourishing ever invented. But without coherent governance, they accelerate inequality and uncertainty.

Technology moves exponentially.
Human systems move linearly.
The gap widens each year.
If we do not align technological innovation with planetary regeneration, the result will be acceleration without direction, a high-speed drift with unpredictable consequences.

The Interconnectedness of Failure

These crises, political, environmental, cultural, technological,

are not separate threads; they are a single fabric.
Pull one thread and the others tighten.
Repair one and the others strengthen.

For example:

- Climate instability drives migration, which destabilises politics.
- Political instability delays climate policy.
- Economic inequality fuels social unrest.
- Social unrest weakens democratic institutions.
- Weak democracies cannot manage technological disruption.

This is why traditional problem-solving has failed.
We have been treating symptoms, not systems.

Where Capital Fits In

Capital is not the only lever, but it is the most catalytic.
Governments can set policy frameworks; communities can demand change; innovators can build new models.
But without capital, intelligent, patient, courageous capital, these possibilities remain theoretical.

The world's greatest challenges are essentially **capital allocation**

problems:

- Which ventures get funded?
- Which technologies scale?
- Which ideas reach the mainstream?
- Which behaviours are rewarded?
- Which industries persist?
- Which systems regenerate or collapse?

When money is misaligned, everything it touches inherits that misalignment.
When money is aligned, regeneration becomes inevitable.

This is why the capital paradox matters: because money is upstream of everything.

A Personal Moment: Seeing the Pattern

I once sat with a founder who had created a technology capable of reducing agricultural water waste by over thirty percent. He had customers, contracts, and proof of concept, everything except the right kind of capital. Venture investors told him it was "too operational." Banks said it was "too early." Grants said it was "too commercial."

He wasn't too early or too niche. He was too *integrated* for a

system that has forgotten how to recognise integration.
He represented the Possible Planet. Capital represented the Current Reality.

That gap, that tragic little gap, is where civilisation loses time, impact, and possibility.

Returning to the Vision - And the Tension

We have seen the Possible Planet.
We have now examined the Current Reality.
The tension between them is not a philosophical exercise, it is the defining challenge of our species.
And yet, this tension has a strange beauty. It contains the seeds of transformation.
Every crisis is a portal.
Every breakdown creates the space for breakthrough.
Every dragon guards a treasure.

The treasure in our time is not gold; it is alignment, the redesign of capital so that it strengthens, rather than strains, the systems that sustain life.

The Question Before Us

If these are the dragons we face…

If these are the failures of our institutions...
If these are the signs of a civilisation between orders...

Then the question becomes inescapable:

What kind of capital system could bridge the gap between our world and the world we could build?

A system that recognises the interconnectedness of our crises.
A system that rewards regeneration as much as return.
A system that operates across the full spectrum of value, financial, ecological, social, cultural.
A system that acknowledges that humanity is not a machine but a living network.

This is where we turn next.
Into the philosophy, frameworks, and architecture that form the *Bridge*, the way across the chasm.

The rest of this book is the construction of that bridge.

CHAPTER 3
THE CRISIS OF MEANING

When a Civilisation Forgets Its "Why"

A Quiet Breaking

There is a quieter crisis unfolding beneath climate change, political polarisation, and economic instability. It is less visible than fires or floods, slower than elections, and harder to quantify than GDP. But it may be more consequential than all of them.

It is the **crisis of meaning**, the slow erosion of the narratives, values, and shared purposes that hold a society together.

Every civilisation depends on an organising story. A shared sense of who we are, what matters, and where we're going. But in recent decades, that story has fractured. We live in a world of unprecedented material abundance and unprecedented spiritual disorientation.

This crisis is not sentimental or abstract. It affects how markets behave, how institutions govern, how communities respond to change, how investors perceive risk, and how young people imagine their futures.

If the Possible Planet is our destination, and the capital paradox is the vehicle malfunction, the crisis of meaning is the **fog that prevents us from seeing the road.**

The Disconnection Epidemic

Around the world, connection is collapsing.
Not digital connection - that is everywhere.
But human connection - the kind that makes life intelligible.
People speak more but understand less.
We are surrounded yet isolated.
We know more and feel less.
We have endless information and diminishing wisdom.

This is not poetic observation; it's measurable.

- Loneliness is at epidemic levels across OECD countries.
- Depression and anxiety are rising in every age cohort.
- Suicide is a leading cause of death among young people.
- Civic participation is declining.
- Trust in institutions, governments, media, corporations, has evaporated.

The paradox is sharp:
We have never been more connected technologically, yet never more disconnected emotionally.

A society without connection becomes a society without coherence and incoherent societies make incoherent decisions.

The Collapse of Shared Reality

Beyond disconnection, we're losing something even more foundational: a shared understanding of the world.

Algorithms fracture newsfeeds.
Politics fractures communities.
Economic inequality fractures empathy.
Hyper-personalised information fractures truth itself.

Two neighbours might live on the same street yet inhabit different realities, consuming different facts, different narratives, different moral frameworks.
A society that does not share reality cannot coordinate action.
A civilisation that cannot coordinate action cannot solve problems.

This is not just a cultural issue - it's a systems issue.
And the dysfunction eventually manifests in everything from climate inaction to investment paralysis.

To solve world-scale problems, we must restore world-scale coherence.
And coherence is a meaning function, not a financial one.

The Myth of Infinite Growth and the Vacuum It Created

For over a century, the dominant narrative of progress was industrial growth.
More output.
More consumption.
More extraction.
More GDP.

Growth gave us comfort and prosperity, but it also concealed a wound:
it reduced meaning to metrics.

When growth became the goal rather than the outcome of healthy systems, we lost our civilisational compass. We mistook expansion for evolution. We confused accumulation with advancement. We equated busyness with purpose.

As the old myths falter, the myth of endless growth, of markets as moral arbiters, of technology as salvation, nothing equally compelling has replaced them.

Humanity is living between stories.
The old story is dying.
The new story is not yet born.
This in-between space is disorienting but it's also fertile.
It is the chrysalis period of civilisation.

Why This Matters for Capital

Capital does not exist in a vacuum.
It flows through the cultural waters of the time.
Meaning shapes markets.

When meaning collapses, capital behaves strangely:

- Investors chase speculative bubbles over long-term assets.
- Institutions optimise for safety over creativity.
- Philanthropists give to symptoms rather than systems.
- Consumers spend to fill emotional voids rather than meet real needs.

- Politicians design policy for news cycles rather than generations.

A meaning-poor society cannot deploy capital well.
A meaning-rich society can transform the world.

This is why values-driven ventures outperform over time, coherence compounds.
And it's why many high-growth ventures with no meaning eventually implode, incoherence compounds as well.

Capital does not just respond to meaning; it amplifies it.

A Personal Reflection: The Founder With the Wrong Story

I once met a founder whose business had every indicator of success, remarkable technology, early revenue, strong customer traction. On paper, he was a dream investment.

But something was wrong.
His team was confused.
His product roadmap zigzagged.
His customers seemed uncertain.

He came to us for capital.
What he needed was a story.

In conversation, it became clear he had no idea *why* he was building his company. The metrics were there, the opportunity was real, but the inner narrative was missing.

Entrepreneurs don't just build products.
They build coherence.
They build meaning.

Once he clarified his purpose, once he understood what problem he was truly solving and for whom, the entire business aligned. His team accelerated, his customers committed, and his capital needs reduced because waste evaporated.

Meaning was the missing infrastructure.

I've seen this pattern again and again.
A founder without meaning burns out.
A company without meaning fractures.
A market without meaning becomes volatile.
A civilisation without meaning becomes unstable.

Meaning as a System Variable

The crisis of meaning is not sentimental despair; it is a systems-level variable.

Wilber framed it as the failure to integrate inner and outer realities.

Spiral Dynamics describes it as the transition from the Green (values-driven but fragmented) to Yellow (integrative, systemic, multi-perspectival).

Anthropologists describe it as a liminal period - the space between narratives.

In this light, the crisis is not a failure.
It is a signal.
Humanity is searching for a deeper coherence.

Integrated Investing responds directly to this.
It aligns the inner (purpose, meaning, values) with the outer (capital design, metrics, governance).
It aligns the individual (founder) with the collective (market).
It aligns short-term outcomes with long-term regeneration.

In other words:
It restores meaning to money.

The Psychological Dimension of Capital

Investors rarely admit it, but the greatest driver of capital misallocation is not risk - it's fear.

- Fear of being first.
- Fear of being wrong.
- Fear of reputational damage.
- Fear of deviating from benchmarks.
- Fear of being seen as idealistic.

Fear shrinks the aperture of possibility.
Courage widens it.

Meaning acts as a stabiliser - it gives investors conviction.
Without meaning, the market oscillates between greed and panic.
With meaning, the market becomes a partner in transformation.

This is why wealth transfer to younger generations is so significant.
Millennials and Gen Z are not more sentimental; they are more *coherent*.
They want investments aligned with identity, values, and the

world they'll inherit.

Meaning is not a fad.
It is the emerging operating system of capitalism.

The Role of Founders in Meaning Reconstruction

Founders are the front line of cultural evolution.
They create the prototypes of the future.
Their ventures model the values society will later normalise.

But founders cannot carry the burden alone.
A founder with a regenerative vision needs capital that shares it.
Otherwise, the tension eventually breaks the company or the founder's spirit.

Integrated investors don't just deploy money.
They deploy meaning.
They fund coherence.

This is what makes the MAD approach different:
Capital as **story architecture**.
Capital as **myth-making infrastructure**.

Capital as **meaning in motion**.

Where This Chapter Leads

If Chapter 1 revealed the structural challenges,
and Chapter 2 mapped the systemic challenges,

Chapter 3 reveals the inner challenges - the heart-mind challenge.

Because unless we redesign meaning, we cannot redesign capital.
Unless we redesign capital, we cannot redesign systems.
Unless we redesign systems, we cannot build the Possible Planet.

The rest of the book will now move into the "Bridge" - the tools and philosophies that reconnect:

- purpose with profit,
- ecology with economy,
- the inner journey with the outer journey,
- the Possible Planet with the present one.

The world is not only starving for capital.

It is starving for coherence.

And coherence is where meaning returns.
Where madness becomes sanity.
And where transformation begins.

CHAPTER 4
WHEN GROWTH STOPPED MEANING PROGRESS

The End of the Old Story

The Myth That Carried a Century

For more than a hundred years, civilisation was propelled by a simple, seductive story: grow the economy and life will get better.

Growth meant prosperity.

Growth meant jobs.

Growth meant stability.

Growth meant progress itself.

It was the story that rebuilt Europe after two world wars, industrialised Asia, lifted billions out of extreme poverty, and delivered comforts previous generations could not imagine. In many ways, it worked.

Until it didn't.

Something subtle but profound has happened over the past several decades: **growth has decoupled from well-being**.
The world grows richer on paper while our ecological foundations erode, political institutions falter, and social health declines.

The story that once united us now obscures the very real limits of a finite planet and a fragile social fabric.

The Linear Illusion

The industrial age taught us to measure progress by how much we could produce.
More steel, more cars, more electricity, more food, more consumption.
The world was a machine; growth was its output.

But our economy was built on a dangerous assumption: that resources were limitless and consequences negligible. GDP, the flagship metric of progress, counts everything except what matters:

- It counts burning forests as economic activity.

- It counts rebuilding after climate disasters as growth.
- It counts medical bills from pollution-induced illness.
- It counts productivity but not play.
- It counts extraction but not regeneration.

GDP is a scoreboard for throughput, not a compass for human flourishing.

When progress becomes quantity instead of quality, we mistake movement for meaning.

Ecological Overshoot: Growth at the Price of Stability

In 1972, the *Limits to Growth* report warned that exponential expansion on a finite planet would eventually hit ecological boundaries. At the time, the idea seemed pessimistic, even radical.

Fifty years later, the data is clear:

- Humanity exceeds six of nine planetary boundaries (Stockholm Resilience Centre, 2023).
- Species extinction rates are now 100–1,000 times above baseline.
- Topsoil is being lost 10 to 40 times faster than it replenishes.

- Freshwater tables are collapsing.
- Oceans are warming and acidifying simultaneously.
- Climate volatility increases the likelihood of simultaneous crop failures, a historically rare event, by more than 400%.

These are not environmental problems.
They are **civilisational risk multipliers**.

Every ecosystem we degrade becomes a debt we must repay with compound interest.

Social Overshoot: When Growth Creates Fragility

The linear-growth story didn't just exceed ecological limits; it exceeded social ones.

Rising GDP alongside declining well-being is not a paradox - it is a warning.

Across OECD nations:

- Life satisfaction has plateaued or declined.
- Loneliness has risen sharply.
- Income inequality has widened to levels not seen since the 1920s.

- Social mobility has stalled; a child's future is increasingly determined by their postcode.
- Economic insecurity persists despite aggregate prosperity.

A society can only tolerate so much asymmetry before the social fabric stretches thin.

People can sense when the story of progress no longer matches their lived reality.

That cognitive-emotional gap becomes political instability.

Political Overshoot: When Growth Fuels Demagoguery

As the growth story decays, so does trust.

Demagogues thrive in the vacuum left by broken narratives.
They offer simplicity where complexity overwhelms.
They promise protection where uncertainty spreads.
They scapegoat where systems are the true cause.

The rise of authoritarianism is not a random cultural shift, it's a symptom of an economic model that still promises endless growth long after its credibility has expired.

When progress stalls, people reach for certainty.
When the future looks unstable, they grasp for the past.

When the centre cannot hold, extremes take root.

The old story is collapsing but the new story is not yet widespread.

Technological Overshoot: Speed Without Direction

Technology accelerates everything, including our confusion.

AI evolves faster than legislation.
Digital platforms scale faster than ethics.
Automation grows faster than re-skilling systems.
Information spreads faster than truth.

We have achieved exponential capability without exponential wisdom.

This is not the fault of technology but of narrative.
In the old story, technology served growth.
In the new story, it must serve regeneration.

Without a coherent vision, even our greatest tools become fuel for instability.

The Hidden Cost of Extraction: The Bill Comes Due

For a century, extraction was the economic model:

- Extract resources from nature.
- Extract productivity from workers.
- Extract attention from citizens.
- Extract returns from future generations.

Extraction generates short-term profit and long-term fragility.

Extraction inflates GDP in the moment it degrades the stability of the systems that make GDP possible.

Extraction is the opposite of stewardship.

When extraction becomes culture, collapse becomes consequence.

A Personal Reflection: When Growth Isn't Growth

Years ago, I met an executive from a multinational company that had seen consistent quarterly growth for over a decade.

Revenue up.

Share price up.

Bonuses up.

But underneath those metrics, something was unwinding.

Employee turnover was rising.

Customer satisfaction was declining.

Product innovation had stalled.

Supplier relationships were fraying.

Environmental compliance fines were increasing.

The company was "growing" but not advancing.

It was expanding, not evolving.

It was extracting, not regenerating.

It was the perfect metaphor for modern capitalism: successful on the scoreboard, weakening on the inside.

What looks like growth on a graph can be decay in reality.

Why the Old Story Persisted

Despite its obvious failures, the growth myth endures for four reasons:

1. **Simplicity:** "More" is easier to measure and understand than "better."
2. **Incentives:** Quarterly earnings reward short timelines; political cycles reward short memories.

3. **Fear:** Challenging the story feels like challenging identity.
4. **Momentum:** Systems continue long after they cease being useful.

The danger is not that the old story is wrong.
The danger is that it no longer serves.

The old story built the world we inherited.
It cannot build the world we need.

The Transition Between Eras

Civilisations do not collapse because they fail.
They collapse because they succeed at one story for too long.

Agrarian societies collapsed when agriculture outstripped ecology.
Industrial societies faltered when machines outpaced meaning.
Digital societies are faltering because connectivity outpaced coherence.

We are transitioning between worldviews:

- from **linear** to **circular**,

- from **extraction** to **regeneration**,
- from **growth** to **integration**,
- from **efficiency** to **coherence**,
- from **fragmentation** to **systems thinking**.

This transition is not optional.
It is inevitable.

The only question is whether we navigate it consciously or by crisis.

Where Capital Fits

Just as growth was the engine of the old story, **capital will be the engine of the new one.**

Capital is how societies vote for the future.
Capital determines which technologies scale, which systems endure, which behaviours proliferate.
Capital is both the steering wheel and the accelerator of civilisation.

If we want to transition from extraction to regeneration, we must transition from:

- capital as fuel

- to capital as design.

From:

- money as an outcome
- to money as an instrument.

From:

- financial returns alone
- to multi-capital returns (natural, social, cultural, intellectual).

This is why the redesign of capital - the Bridge - must follow immediately after the diagnosis of collapse.

The Need for a New Story

Growth is no longer a sufficient story.
It tells us where we've been, not where we're going.
It tells us what we measure, not what we value.
It tells us how to extract, not how to restore.

What we need now is a story capable of integrating:

- ecology and economy,

- technology and ethics,
- individual aspiration and collective stewardship,
- financial logic and planetary logic.

The story we need is the story of **integration**.

And integrated investing is not a technical innovation - it is a narrative one.
It is the story that says:

"We can prosper while healing.
We can grow by regenerating.
We can create value by creating coherence."

It is the story of the Possible Planet made practical.

Setting the Stage for the Bridge

With this chapter, the descent into the Current Reality is complete.
We have examined:

- capital misalignment (Chapter 1),
- systemic instability (Chapter 2),
- the crisis of meaning (Chapter 3),
- the end of the growth story (Chapter 4).

Now we stand at civilisation's threshold, the same threshold that defines every Hero's Journey.

This is where the Bridge begins.
Where philosophy becomes architecture.
Where hope becomes design.
Where vision becomes method.

Chapter 5 will introduce the origin of MAD and the emergence of **Integrated Investing**, the new story, the new architecture, and the new operating system for capital.

Because if the old story of growth has expired, then a new story must rise, one worthy of the world we could build.
And that story begins with MAD.

CHAPTER 5
THE ORIGIN OF MAD

From Operators to Architects of Capital

The Moment the Old Tools Stopped Working

Every meaningful transformation begins with a moment of recognition, a moment when the old ways stop making sense, when the tools that once built success no longer fit the shape of the problem.

For years, we had been founders, operators, and builders. We had scaled companies in multiple industries, raised capital in good markets and bad, navigated mergers, exits, implosions, turnarounds, partnerships, breakthroughs, and failures. We'd lived inside the machinery of business: cash flow, culture, product, people, the invisible threads founders must hold while everything around them grows more complex.

We knew what it took to build something that mattered. And we knew what it felt like when the capital you needed, the right capital, at the right time, with the right intention, simply did not exist.

There was a point where the pattern became undeniable. It didn't matter whether the founder was building regenerative agriculture systems or clean energy networks or new education models, the struggle was the same. The companies doing the *real* work of repairing and reimagining the world were starved of aligned capital. Meanwhile, capital seemed to flow effortlessly toward ventures that solved trivial problems for affluent consumers.

Something was wrong with the system.
Not at the margins. At the core.

We realised the greatest bottleneck in human progress wasn't innovation.
It was **the architecture of capital itself**.

When Experience Becomes Insight

There's a reason operators often become better investors than investors become operators: you learn to see the connective tissue of a business, the parts no spreadsheet or pitch deck can ever fully capture.

The Origin of MAD

You see how culture determines velocity.
You see how leadership determines resilience.
You see how timing determines destiny.
And you see how capital, when misaligned, can break even the most brilliant team.

We had been inside enough ventures to recognise a painful truth:

Many founders fail not because their ideas are wrong, but because their capital is.

Capital that extracts too early.
Capital that grows too fast.
Capital that demands the wrong metrics.
Capital that warps incentives.
Capital that mistakes potential for certainty.
Capital that confuses speculation with stewardship.

We had seen ventures implode not from weakness, but from the wrong kind of money.

The reverse was also true:
When a founder receives capital that matches their stage, values, market reality, and growth rhythm, they become

unstoppable.

This wasn't theoretical. It was observable.
It was repeatable.
It was universal across sectors.

And it led us to a simple, almost obvious question:

What if capital itself could be redesigned?
Not just deployed more wisely, *redesigned structurally* to create better outcomes for founders, investors, and society at the same time?

The MAD Realisation

MAD began long before the name existed.
It began as a pattern of frustration, a sense that the world's best ideas were trapped behind the world's worst incentives.

But the real turning point came from a single insight:

"Solving humanity's biggest problems *is* humanity's biggest economic opportunity."

The world wasn't short of opportunity; it was short of alignment.

Impact wasn't a side quest; it was a structural economic tailwind.
Regeneration wasn't an ideal; it was a competitive advantage.
Purpose wasn't sentimental; it was a strategy.

And the companies building these futures needed a new kind of partner, not financiers, but **co-creators**.

They needed capital that understood complexity.
Capital that had built things before.
Capital that valued coherence over hype.
Capital that could listen to founders and see both their wounds and their genius.
Capital that knew what it felt like to meet payroll on Thursday with nothing in the bank on Tuesday.

In short: they needed *operator capital* - capital informed by lived experience.

That was the genesis of MAD:
operators choosing to become architects of capital, because no one else was building the structures the future required.

The Name That Named Us

At first it was half a joke.

"Maybe you need to be a little mad to build something that actually matters."

The line kept returning. Because there was truth in it.

MAD didn't stand for madness.
It stood for **Make A Difference** - but the double meaning was perfect.

To make a difference, you often have to challenge the consensus.
To change the world, you sometimes have to break the rules.
To build the Possible Planet, you must reject the idea that the present is unchangeable.
And to reimagine capital, you must ignore the voices saying "This is how it's always been done."

Yes - it *is* a little mad.
But in a world this broken, sanity looks like surrender.
MAD became our name because it captured both the mission and the spirit:
practical idealism with the courage of the unreasonable.

The Philosophy Beneath the Name

MAD was not built as a fund.

It was built as a **philosophy**, a worldview about how money, meaning, and systems interact.

Four convictions shape that philosophy:

1. Business is the most scalable tool humans have ever invented.
Governments influence, charities alleviate, but business *scales*.
When done consciously, it becomes a regenerative engine.

2. Capital is the bloodstream of civilisation.
If the blood is toxic, even a healthy body becomes sick.
If capital becomes regenerative, everything it touches becomes regenerative.

3. Founders are the immune system of society.
They respond to what is broken, create what is missing, and adapt faster than institutions.

4. The future belongs to integrated thinkers.
Those who can hold financial logic and ecological logic, market forces and human psychology, data and meaning – simultaneously - will build the next economy.

MAD exists because the world needs investors who think like founders and founders who understand systems.

It needs capital that behaves like a partner, not a predator.

The Founders We Met - And the Pattern That Emerged

As we began meeting companies intentionally, founders across agritech, climate tech, health tech, education, water, waste, and circular economy, the pattern sharpened:

- The biggest opportunities were in solving real systemic problems.
- The most interesting founders were motivated by mission, not ego.
- The most profitable business models were inherently regenerative.
- And the capital these founders needed simply did not exist.

Either the money was:

- too bureaucratic,
- too extractive,
- too impatient,
- too slow,

- too ignorant of operational reality,
- or too scared of anything that didn't promise a hockey stick graph.

We saw that founders didn't just need capital.
They needed **navigation, pattern recognition,** and **philosophical grounding**.

They needed the Venture Compass™ - though it didn't have that name yet.

The MAD Compass Moment

The Compass emerged gradually, a synthesis of 40+ years of combined experience.

It was built around one truth:
Every venture exists inside an ecosystem.

So, we mapped the eight forces that consistently determine whether a company grows, stalls, or collapses:

1. **Market Validation**
2. **Market Forces**
3. **Growth Model**
4. **Capital Strategy**

5. **Structure**
6. **Culture**
7. **People**
8. **Impact**

Impact - Point 8 - wasn't tacked on as a moral flourish.
It was embedded as the final diagnostic of coherence.
If a company's success damages the world, its cost of capital will eventually destroy it.

The Compass gave us a shared language for evaluating founders with fairness and precision.
And it became the backbone of the MAD method.

The Bridge Philosophy Takes Shape

At this point we had:

- a philosophy (integration),
- a diagnostic (the Compass),
- a purpose (Make A Difference),
- and a clear gap in the market (aligned growth capital).

What we needed next was **a structural expression** of this worldview -
a way to channel capital consistently, coherently, and at scale.

This led to the architecture that would eventually become:

- the MAD Hyperscalers Fund (with structured yield + equity),
- and the Integrated Impact Model.

But beneath the architecture was a deeper idea:

Capital is a design problem.
The world we get is the world we finance.

If we redesign money, we redesign everything money touches.

And money touches everything.

Why MAD Had to Exist

MAD wasn't formed because we wanted to be fund managers. MAD was formed because **a void existed** - a void that had consequences.

Without capital that understands purpose, purposeful founders fail.
When purposeful founders fail, systemic solutions don't scale.

When systemic solutions don't scale, crises accelerate.

There was no point waiting for incumbents to wake up.
The future needed a new kind of capital - now.

MAD stepped into that void with a simple but radical belief:

You can build a better civilisation by building better companies and financing them with better capital.
Not theory.
Practice.
Operator-led, system-aware, purpose-aligned practice.

The MAD Ethos: Courage Over Convention

MAD's ethos rests on one question:

"What would you do if you were not afraid?"

Most of the world's problems persist not because solutions don't exist,
but because courage is scarce.

MAD exists to demonstrate that courage can be engineered, through philosophy, through capital design, through alignment, and through community.

To be MAD is to act with:

- clarity rather than certainty,
- courage rather than compliance,
- coherence rather than convention,
- imagination rather than inertia.

This ethos is the energy of integrated investing, a capitalism mature enough to hold complexity and compassionate enough to act on it.

Closing the Origin Story: Crossing the Threshold

If the first four chapters mapped the descent - the world's fragmentation, the collapse of the old story, the failures of the current system - then Chapter 5 is the moment the Hero crosses the threshold.

The call has been answered.
The tools have been discovered.
The journey into the Bridge begins.

From here, the book moves into the architecture of

transformation:

- The Compass
- Integrated Investing
- Regenerative Capital
- The MAD Hyperscalers Fund
- The Amplifier Model
- Case studies
- And the practicalities of designing the Possible Planet.

The origin of MAD is the origin of possibility - proof that courage, design, and capital can meet in the same place and build something worthy of the age.

PART II
THE BRIDGE

CHAPTER 6
THE VENTURE COMPASS

Navigation for Growth With Integrity

A Map for the Unknown

Every meaningful journey requires a way of seeing. Founders do not walk straight, predictable paths. They walk spirals, climbs, falls, breakthroughs, false summits and sudden descents. Markets shift without warning. Competitors appear unexpectedly. Customers evolve faster than business plans. The Venture Compass was born inside this reality. It was not designed in theory. It was distilled from operating experience, from watching founders succeed and fail, often for reasons that traditional investors never even perceived.

Again and again we saw the same truth. The companies that succeeded were not the ones with the most perfect pitch deck or the most polished spreadsheets. They were the companies with coherence. Their internal architecture matched the external environment. Their people, culture, strategy and capital were aligned. Their purpose and their product spoke the same language.

And the companies that struggled were not always the ones with flawed ideas. Often, they had potential that was never realised because the forces that shaped them pulled in different directions. They were misaligned.

The Compass was created to understand these forces. It is not a checklist. It is a way of seeing. It is a multidimensional map that reveals what a company is, what it can become and what must happen to close the distance between those two states.

The Venture Compass has eight primary forces. Then, at the centre, a ninth force that gives the whole model life. And beneath all of them, the most important dimension of all, the Gap between current reality and potential, and what it will take to close it.

Let us walk through the eight visible forces first.

1. Market Validation, the truth of demand

Market Validation asks the most fundamental question of all, does the world want this?

Not would they like it.

Not would they talk about it.
Not would they pilot it.
But would they pay for it, adopt it, use it repeatedly and weave it into their behaviour.

Validation is the gravitational proof of a real market.
It is behavioural, not conceptual.

It answers:

- Is the problem painful enough?
- Will customers pay real money to solve it?
- Is usage consistent and predictable?
- Is retention evidence of value, not inertia?

Validation determines whether a venture is building for reality or for imagination.

When Market Validation is strong, growth has foundation.
When it is weak, everything else is fragile.

2. Market Forces, the winds that shape growth

No company grows in isolation. Every business is shaped by external forces that push, pull or destabilise.

Market Forces include:

- regulatory headwinds
- cultural trends
- technological cost curves
- demographic shifts
- supply chain dynamics
- competitor behaviour
- macro cycles

To scale, founders must understand their environment.
To surf a wave, you must see the wave.

Market Forces reveal whether a market will carry a company or crush it, whether the venture is swimming upstream or moving with the current.

3. Growth Model, the engine of expansion

A company is not a product. It is an engine. And engines have mechanics. They have inputs and outputs, friction points and acceleration points, conversion rates, cost structures, retention patterns and expansion levers.

The Growth Model answers:

- How do we acquire customers?

- What does that cost?
- How long do they stay?
- What drives revenue expansion?
- Where do margins strengthen or erode?
- Where does scale create leverage, or create chaos?

Without a coherent growth model, capital amplifies disorder. With one, capital amplifies destiny.

Growth is never magic. It is mechanics.

4. Capital Strategy, the right money at the right time

Capital is often treated as generic, but money is never generic. It always comes with shape, intention, timing, expectations and structural implications.

A Capital Strategy answers:

- How much capital?
- At what moment?
- From what source?
- In what structure?
- At what valuation?
- Linked to what milestones?

The wrong capital at the wrong time can destroy a venture.

The right capital at the right time can transform it.

Founders need not just capital, but congruence.

5. Structure, the architecture that holds everything

Structure includes every invisible element that determines stability and scalability:

- legal configuration
- governance
- operational rhythm
- unit economics
- pricing mechanics
- supply chains
- incentive systems
- financial architecture
- product sequencing

Structure is not glamorous, but it is destiny.
It is the frame that holds growth.

Most companies fail structurally long before they fail strategically.

6. Culture, the emotional infrastructure

Culture is the most underestimated force in business. It is not the values on the wall, but the values in use. It is what happens when pressure is applied.

Culture reveals:

- how people tell the truth
- how conflict is handled
- what behaviour is tolerated
- how decisions are made
- what people fear
- where people stretch and where they shrink
- how the team speaks, listens and repairs

Culture determines whether growth amplifies the mission or erodes it.

You cannot out-strategise a broken culture.
You can only rebuild it.

7. People, the human vectors of the venture

People are not resources. They are vectors, each with direction, momentum, energy and influence. A company's future depends not only on what people know, but on who they are becoming.

The Compass evaluates:

- founder psychology
- leadership maturity
- succession logic
- skill distribution
- emotional intelligence
- behavioural patterns
- conflict style
- resilience under pressure

Businesses scale not on their ideas, but on their people.

8. Impact, the coherence between growth and the world

Impact is not a moral accessory. It is a structural force.

Impact asks:

- Does the company regenerate or deplete the systems it touches?

- Does each dollar of revenue correspond to a net positive effect?
- Does the business model align with planetary boundaries?
- Does success create resilience or risk?
- Does growth strengthen community, culture or ecology?

Impact is last in the eight because it is the result of the others. It reflects whether the entire architecture is coherent or corrosive.

Impact is not a badge. It is a consequence.

The Ninth Dimension, the X Factor

Only after the eight forces are understood does the ninth reveal itself. It lives at the centre of the Compass. It is the integrative field that gives the model depth.

We call it the X Factor.

The X Factor is the invisible quality that emerges when the whole is greater than the sum of its parts. It is difficult to describe, but unmistakable when present. It is not mystical in the sense of irrational, but mystical in the sense that it arises from patterns that are deeper than metrics.

The X Factor is:

- the coherence of the story
- the founder's alignment with mission
- the felt integrity of decisions
- the way culture carries energy
- the trust that moves through the team
- the clarity that appears at moments of pressure
- the intuitive knowing that guides direction

It is the difference between a competent company and an inevitable one.

Intuition and the quantum leap

Intuition is the hidden engine of the X Factor. Harvard Business Review once wrote that analysis is the ceiling of management, but intuition is the leap into leadership. Management sees what is. Leadership senses what is emerging.

Intuition lets founders:

- pivot before the data becomes obvious
- hear the truth beneath customer words
- recruit the right people without perfect information
- feel timing
- see patterns where others see noise

Intuition does not replace analysis, it elevates it.

The X Factor is that elevation.

The Compass Gap, where ROI truly lives

If the eight forces reveal what a company is, and the X Factor reveals what it feels like, the Gap reveals something deeper:

what the company could become, and what it will cost to get there.

The Compass measures two states across every dimension:

- Current Reality
- Potential

The Gap is the difference between the two.

This is the most powerful and least understood part of the

Compass. It turns the model from a diagnostic into a forecasting engine.

What the Gap reveals

The Gap tells us:

- how much transformation is required
- where the major unlocks are
- how much capital is truly needed
- how long transformation will take
- what capability gaps exist
- where failure risk concentrates
- where acceleration is possible
- what the real ROI could be

This shifts investing from speculation to design.

The Gap as ROI predictor

Traditional ROI estimates look at capital inputs and predicted financial outputs. That model is incomplete.

MAD calculates ROI from the shape and cost of closing the Gap.

A narrow Gap may require little capital and deliver high return.
A wide but bridgeable Gap, if matched with the right team and support, may yield extraordinary return.
A wide and misaligned Gap may show that even large capital will not create transformation.
An enormous aligned Gap may signal a once in a generation opportunity.

Return is not created by capital alone.
Return is created by the closing of the Gap.

It takes a village to raise a company

Closing the Gap requires more than money. Capital is only one ingredient. Transformation requires capability, wisdom, perspective, guidance and experience. It requires the collective intelligence of people who have walked the path before.

This is why MAD built an ecosystem rather than a fund.
We assembled a group of more than thirty Ambassadors, each with deep expertise, lived experience, networks and a shared desire to make a difference on the planet.

The proverb is true. It takes a village to raise a child. It also takes a village to raise a company.

The MAD village brings:

- pattern recognition
- strategic clarity
- operational guidance
- emotional support
- industry introductions
- cultural insight
- systems thinking
- problem solving
- founder development
- narrative coherence
- global perspective

This village does something capital alone cannot do. It closes the Gap faster, with less friction, with less wasted time, with less wasted money and with far greater coherence.

The synergistic benefit

When the Compass, the X Factor and the Gap are combined with the MAD ecosystem, the result is a powerful synergy:

- companies grow with integrity

- founders evolve faster
- capital is deployed more intelligently
- time to scale reduces
- risk reduces
- impact intensifies
- resilience increases
- investor returns improve
- and the mission accelerates

The village becomes the amplifier.
The Compass becomes the map.
The Gap becomes the path.
The X Factor becomes the energy.
Capital becomes the catalyst.

Together they form a coherent system for building ventures that make a difference on the planet.

Where the Compass leads next

The Compass prepares the mind and reveals the truth of the venture. The Gap prepares the strategy and reveals the cost of transformation. The X Factor prepares the intuition and reveals the company's future arc.

All of this points toward the next chapter, the philosophical foundation that ties everything together.

To build the Possible Planet, we must integrate financial performance, human purpose, ecological boundaries and cultural meaning. That integration is the evolution beyond impact.

Chapter 7 is where that story begins.

CHAPTER 7
INTEGRATION BEYOND IMPACT

The Evolution of Capital Consciousness

When "Impact" Lost Its Meaning

Impact investing began with noble ambition. It was the first attempt in modern finance to unite capital with conscience, profit with purpose, economics with empathy. In its early years, it felt revolutionary. It challenged the assumption that markets were morally neutral. It proposed that return and responsibility could coexist.

But over time, something happened.
Impact fractured.
Impact diluted.
Impact became a category, then a checkbox, then a marketing strategy.

Today, much of what passes for impact investing is simply conventional investing with softer language. ESG screens,

SDG logos and ethical overlays create the illusion of coherence without altering the underlying logic of extractive finance.

Impact became a destination when it should have been a doorway.
It became a badge when it should have been a bridge.
It became static when the world required dynamism.

This is not to dismiss the field. Impact investing did crucial work. It created the language that allowed a generation to think differently. But language without architecture cannot scale.
What we need now is not more impact, but **more integration**.

Integration, the Next Evolution

Integrated investing is not a category.
It is a worldview.

It begins with a simple premise:

A company is not separate from the world it inhabits.
A market is not separate from the systems that sustain it.
And capital is not separate from the consequences it creates.

Integration means recognising that financial, social, cultural and ecological capital are interdependent. Separate them, and all become fragile. Integrate them, and all become generative.

Integration is what impact was trying to point toward, but could not fully articulate.

Impact asks, "What good does this create?"
Integration asks, "What system does this strengthen?"

Impact measures outcomes.
Integration measures coherence.

Impact looks at metrics.
Integration looks at meaning.

Impact validates behaviour.
Integration transforms behaviour.

Impact is quantitative.
Integration is multidimensional.
Impact can be siloed.
Integration cannot.

The Four Dimensions of Integration

Integrated investing unites four domains that traditional finance treats as separate:

1. Inner Reality
Values, intuition, motivation, founder psychology, leadership maturity.
This is the realm of why.

2. Outer Reality
Markets, capital flows, governance, macro forces.
This is the realm of what.

3. Individual Reality
Personal agency, strategic choices, resilience, skill and capability.
This is the realm of who.

4. Collective Reality
Culture, community, ecosystem dynamics, planetary boundaries.
This is the realm of where.

When these are aligned, a venture becomes coherent.
When they fracture, even the strongest ideas collapse.

This four-quadrant integration comes directly from Ken Wilber's Integral Theory, which argues that any complex system can only be understood when inner and outer, individual and collective perspectives are held together. Remove any quadrant, and your understanding becomes incomplete.

Impact investing traditionally focused on the LR quadrant (outer-collective): systems, policies, outcomes.
Integrated investing pulls all four quadrants into a single frame.

This is why it works.

Spiral Dynamics and the Evolution of Capital

If Integral Theory gives us the architecture, Spiral Dynamics gives us the psychology.

Spiral Dynamics describes how human values and worldviews evolve through predictable stages. Two stages matter most here:

- **Green**, the impact era

- Values-driven, ethical, emotionally aware, but often fragmented and idealistic.
- **Yellow**, the integrative era
- Systemic, multidimensional, pragmatic, capable of holding paradox, grounded in complexity.

Impact investing grew from Green consciousness.
Integrated investing emerges from Yellow.

Green tries to fix problems with more compassion.
Yellow redesigns systems so the problems do not arise.

Green fights symptoms.
Yellow integrates root causes.

Green adds ethical layers to the old model.
Yellow rewrites the model from the inside out.
Integrated investing is Yellow finance, a leap in perspective rather than an iteration of impact.

Planetary Boundaries, the Science of Limits

Integration is not philosophical alone. It is scientific.

The Planetary Boundaries framework, developed by the

Stockholm Resilience Centre, identifies nine ecological thresholds humanity must live within to maintain a stable Earth system. We are currently exceeding six of those boundaries.

Integrated investing recognises that companies do not operate outside these planetary constraints. They operate inside them. A business model that depends on breaching boundaries is not merely unethical. It is economically suicidal.

Planetary Boundaries become design constraints. They guide product development, capital deployment and strategy creation. They move "impact" from aspiration to engineering.

When a venture grows inside boundaries, risk declines and resilience rises.
When a venture grows by breaching boundaries, both collapse.

Integration turns the biosphere into the balance sheet.

The Zeitz 4Cs, Culture as a Capital Asset

Jochen Zeitz, co founder of the B Team and architect of regenerative capitalism, created the 4Cs framework as a foundation for holistic value creation.

The 4Cs are:

- Conservation
- Community
- Culture
- Commerce

Most impact frameworks measure Commerce and Conservation.
Few measure Culture and Community.
Integration measures all four.

Culture and Community are not soft concepts. They are economic multipliers. Healthy communities create stable demand. Strong culture attracts talent, trust and longevity. These translate directly into margin, retention and customer lifetime value.

Integrated investing incorporates the 4Cs because regeneration is not solely ecological. It is relational.

Integration in Action, Purpose as Strategy

When integrated investing is practiced, companies make

decisions differently.

A founder evaluating a new product does not ask "Will this sell?"
They ask "Will this create coherence across system, culture, and planet?"

A board evaluating strategy does not ask "What is the projected IRR?"
They ask "What is the long term resilience profile of this value creation?"

An investor evaluating a deal does not ask "What is the upside?"
They ask "What will it cost the world for this company to grow?"

Integration does not reject financial return.
It deepens it.

It asks for returns that are:

- durable
- resilient

- systemic
- multi capital
- long horizon
- regenerative

These returns prove more valuable than hypergrowth that collapses.

Integration and the Venture Compass

The Venture Compass is built on integrated logic.

- Market Validation connects with outer reality.
- Culture and People connect with inner reality.
- Market Forces and Structure connect with collective reality.
- Impact and X Factor connect with meaning and emergence.

Integrated investing is the philosophy that makes the Compass intelligible as a system.

Without integration, the Compass is a diagnostic.

With integration, it becomes a navigation tool for systems transformation.

Integration is what turns eight forces and a ninth dimension into a living map of possibility.

The MAD Integrated Impact Model

MAD's integrated approach brings together:

- UN SDGs
- Planetary Boundaries
- Zeitz 4Cs
- Venture Compass diagnostics
- Multi capital accounting
- Founder narrative and psychology
- Cultural coherence
- ROI of gap closure
- Systems and relational intelligence

This is why our model moves beyond ESG or simple impact. It does not measure isolated metrics. It measures systems alignment.

The model is not a report.
It is a worldview expressed operationally.

It tells us:

- what a company contributes
- what it consumes
- what it repairs
- what it transforms
- and what future it is building

Integrated investing is not soft. It is precise. It is as concerned with biodiversity as with customer retention, as attentive to narrative coherence as to EBITDA.

In this worldview, finance is not independent of the world. It is embedded in it.

Why Integration Outperforms Extraction

Extraction seeks short term gain, often at long term cost. Integration seeks long term value by strengthening the system itself.

Extraction scales fragility.
Integration scales resilience.

Extraction produces waste.
Integration produces regeneration.

Extraction externalises cost.

Integration internalises responsibility.

Extraction burns trust.
Integration compounds it.

Markets are beginning to recognise this. Investors who think in decades rather than quarters are quietly moving toward integrative logic. The data increasingly shows that companies aligned with integrated principles outperform over the long term.

Integrated companies:

- attract better talent
- recover faster from shocks
- enjoy stronger customer loyalty
- produce more consistent returns
- receive cheaper capital
- experience lower regulatory risk
- innovate more effectively
- and become harder to disrupt

Integration is not idealism. It is competitive advantage.

A Personal Reflection, The Moment Integration Became Obvious

There was a moment when all of this crystallised for me. I was sitting with a founder working on a regenerative agriculture platform. Their revenue was steady, their margins predictable, their impact meaningful. But they were struggling to attract capital because they were not a "hot category".

What struck me was the absurdity.
This was a business solving food security, soil health, and climate resilience.
The unit economics were healthy.
The demand was growing.
The risk profile was lower than the average SaaS company.

But the market could not see it because the market was not trained to see systems.

In that moment, I realised that until capital becomes integrated, the world will continue to misallocate opportunity. Integration does not just create better returns. It reveals them.

Integration as the Bridge

Integration is the bridge between the Possible Planet and the current one. It holds together all the dimensions we have explored so far:

- the vision of what humanity could be
- the reality of the crises we face
- the failures of the growth paradigm
- the need for a new story
- the birth of MAD
- the intelligence of the Compass
- the intuition of the X Factor
- the transformation pathway revealed by the Gap
- the ecosystem that closes that Gap
- and the structural design of capital that aligns purpose with performance

Integration is the worldview that turns these elements into a system rather than a collection of ideas.

The Invitation to Integrate

Integration is not something investors "apply" to companies. It is a way of being.

It asks of us:

- deeper listening
- broader awareness
- longer time horizons
- multidimensional thinking

- courage to act across silos
- clarity of purpose
- humility in complexity
- creativity in constraint

Integration is the maturity of capital.
It is finance grown up.

Where Integration Leads

The rest of this book now moves into **the architecture** of integrated investing:

- how to structure capital for regeneration
- how MAD designed its funds
- how the Amplifier model works
- how philanthropy multiplies private investment
- how founders evolve in integrated systems
- and how we build the Possible Planet through the bridge of integrated capital

Integration is the philosophy.
The next chapters are the engineering.

We have the map.
We have the worldview.

Now we begin building the new operating system of capital.

CHAPTER 8
THE ARCHITECTURE OF MAD CAPITAL

Designing Money for a Regenerative Future

Capital Is Not Neutral

Every civilisation expresses itself through the way it allocates resources. Feudal societies allocated through lineage. Agrarian societies allocated through land. Industrial societies allocated through labour and production. The digital age allocates through information and networks.

Across all eras, one truth holds steady:
capital shapes civilisation.

In the old paradigm, capital was designed for extraction.
It pulled value toward the few.
It measured success in quarters, not generations.
It rewarded scale without substance and pressure without purpose.

If we are to build the Possible Planet, the architecture of

capital must evolve.

It must support regeneration rather than depletion.

It must strengthen the systems that sustain life.

It must propagate coherence, not fragmentation.

MAD exists to design that capital.

The Philosophy Beneath the Architecture

Before structuring a dollar, we asked a deeper question:

What kind of capital would a regenerative world require?

Such capital would need to be:

- aligned with founders, not adversarial,
- patient in timing, urgent in purpose,
- capable of generating real cash returns,
- able to scale ventures solving human and planetary problems,
- flexible enough to integrate philanthropy, private capital and policy,
- and designed around transformation, not speculation.

Capital is not passive. It is formative.

The MAD Hyperscalers Fund is the structural expression of this philosophy.

It is not three funds.

It is one fund built on **three founding principles**:

1. **Capital fit for purpose**
2. **Scale-ready structured capital**
3. **Philanthropy as catalyst**

Together they create a unified architecture we call **Regenerative Capital Design**.

Founding Principle One
Capital Fit for Purpose
Funding that strengthens, not distorts, the company
Early-scale businesses face a unique dilemma. They have revenue, customers and validation, but lack capital structured to match their growth rhythm. Traditional equity demands dilution. Venture demands hypergrowth. Bank debt demands collateral. Grants lack persistence. Each creates distortion.

MAD's first founding principle solves this with **capital designed for fit**:

- structured capital aligned to free cash flow,
- modest equity to align incentives without stripping ownership,

- repayment mechanics matched to operational reality,
- founder friendly terms that protect mission and pace,
- and strategic support that reduces risk before capital increases scale.

This principle acknowledges two truths:

1. **Dilution is expensive.**
2. **Misaligned capital destabilises companies.**

Fit-for-purpose capital strengthens a company's capacity to grow without warping the mission or overwhelming the team. It is fuel that matches the engine.

This is built directly into the MAD Hyperscalers Fund.

Founding Principle Two
Scale-Ready Structured Capital
Designing money to accelerate momentum, resilience and impact
Where the first principle ensures alignment, the second ensures **scalability.**

Structured capital with an equity upside component allows the fund to:

- provide consistent quarterly distributions,
- build resilience in investor returns,
- maintain founder alignment,
- support companies with recurring revenue,
- and promote long-term success over short-term speculation.

This principle reduces reliance on the "unicorn outcome," and rewards companies that demonstrate:

- capital efficiency,
- recurring revenue,
- system positive outcomes,
- operational maturity,
- and alignment with planetary and community boundaries.

Rather than chasing improbable extremes,
the MAD Hyperscalers Fund scales companies that solve essential problems and already demonstrate traction.

It is **momentum based**, not fantasy based.
Resilience based, not volatility based.
Regenerative, not extractive.

Founding Principle Three
Philanthropy as Catalyst
Small contributions unlocking large-scale capital flows

The third founding principle is catalytic capital.
MAD's insight was simple:

"If philanthropy absorbs early risk, private capital accelerates, and systems shift faster."

A small catalytic layer, contributed through philanthropic partners or mission aligned supporters:

- de-risks the structure,
- increases investor confidence,
- attracts institutional and government co-funding,
- accelerates deployment,
- amplifies outcomes,
- and multiplies the impact of every dollar.

Philanthropy stops acting as charity.
It becomes the **ignition mechanism** that unlocks large-scale private capital.

In this model:

- philanthropy catalyses speed,
- structured capital ensures stability,
- equity delivers upside,
- and together they create a regenerative capital engine.

This catalytic principle is part of the single MAD Hyperscalers Fund,
not a separate vehicle and it is one of the reasons MAD's architecture is uniquely positioned to address global problems at scale.

One Fund, Three Principles, One System

These three founding principles are not separate pools of money.

They are the design code of the **MAD Hyperscalers Fund** - a fund built to carry ventures from validation, through early scale, into national and global momentum.

The Hyperscalers Fund is not only capital.
It is *capital engineered for coherence*.
Together, the principles allow MAD to:

- preserve founder ownership,
- accelerate investor returns,
- reduce risk,

- increase resilience,
- amplify system level impact,
- and shorten the time required for transformation.

It is a capital architecture designed not only to grow companies,
but to grow the Possible Planet.

How the Architecture Closes the Gap

In Chapter 6, we explored the Gap - the distance between a company's current reality and its potential across the eight Compass forces.

The three founding principles of the MAD Hyperscalers Fund exist *specifically to close that gap*:

- Fit-for-purpose capital supports alignment.
- Structured capital supports scale.
- Philanthropic catalysis supports acceleration.

But capital alone cannot close the gap.

Closing the gap requires **capability**, not only cash.
It requires the right people, sequence, culture, leadership and network.

It requires the "village."

The Village That Raises a Company

MAD's capital design is embedded inside a broader ecosystem, anchored by:

- more than 30 Ambassadors,
- seasoned operators,
- technologists,
- founders,
- cultural leaders,
- impact pioneers,
- storytellers,
- global connectors,
- and regenerative thinkers.

This collective intelligence surrounds each investment to:

- reduce risk,
- stretch leadership,
- compress time,
- solve blockages,
- refine strategy,
- strengthen culture,
- accelerate product,

- expand networks,
- and amplify resilience.

The proverb is true.

It takes a village to raise a child.

It also takes a village to raise a company.

The village shortens the journey.

The village increases ROI.

The village strengthens impact.

The village reduces burn.

The village multiplies outcomes.

The village makes the transformation possible.

Capital is a lever.

Community is the multiplier.

Regenerative Capital Architecture in Practice

When these principles work together inside one fund and one ecosystem, they produce:

- consistent cash returns for investors,
- stronger and more resilient companies,
- faster scaling of solutions to global problems,
- deeper founder development,

- reduced capital wastage,
- greater impact per dollar,
- and more coherent, durable value.

MAD does not operate like traditional venture.
MAD does not operate like philanthropy.
MAD does not operate like private credit.

MAD is an integrated system.

It is capital redesigned for a world in transition.

Why Structure Is the Final Form of Philosophy

Philosophy shapes intention.
Intention shapes structure.
Structure shapes behaviour.
Behaviour shapes outcomes.
Outcomes shape civilisation.

In designing the MAD Hyperscalers Fund,
we were not only designing a finance vehicle.
We were designing a worldview expressed as mathematics.
A philosophy expressed as economics.
A belief expressed as structure.
When you design capital well,

you design the conditions for a better future.

The Bridge to What Comes Next

The first half of this book described the need.

Chapters 5 to 8 have described the response:

the origin, the map, the worldview and the architecture that make integrated investing possible.

What comes next is the journey across the bridge.

We now turn to the *mechanics* of transformation:

- how the Compass moves strategy,
- how gaps are closed,
- how capital and capability intertwine,
- how outcomes compound,
- and how companies achieve scale through coherence.

The next chapter steps into this terrain.

CHAPTER 9
ENGINEERING REPEATABLE OUTCOMES

How Transformation Becomes Predictable

The Myth of the "Unpredictable Venture"

Most investors and founders speak about venture as if it were a roulette wheel, a game of chance where success is mysterious and failure is fate. Phrases like "venture is a numbers game" or "you just need one outlier" are repeated as if they were laws of physics. This mythology is convenient, because it absolves investors of responsibility. When outcomes appear random, no one is accountable for understanding failure patterns.

But the truth is different.

Venture outcomes are not random.

They are patterns.

And patterns can be understood, influenced and engineered.

The MAD philosophy is built on a simple belief:

"If you understand the system, you can predict the path. If you can predict the path, you can design the outcome."

When you design capital, capability, culture and leadership together, outcomes become repeatable.
Not guaranteed, but intentionally shaped.

This is the heart of integrated investing.
It turns "chance" into "design."

Why Most Venture Models Fail to Scale Purpose

Traditional venture capital is structured around three flawed assumptions:

1. **Hypergrowth equals success.**
2. This ignores timing, market readiness, culture and systems capacity.
3. **The portfolio will self-correct.**
4. This allows weak companies to fester and strong companies to burn out.
5. **Intervention is minimal.**
6. VC firms often add "advice" rather than leadership, capability or systemic support.

These assumptions create a landscape where nine of ten companies fail, and the tenth must be extraordinary to pay for the others. Failure becomes "expected," which is shorthand for "accepted."

MAD rejects this logic.
Failure should not be expected; it should be understood.
Success should not be accidental; it should be engineered.

The Compass, the X Factor, the Gap and the architecture of capital create the foundation.
MAD's ecosystem creates the repetition.

The Three Levers of Repeatable Success

Repeatable outcomes come from three tightly integrated levers:

1. **Coherence** - alignment across all eight Compass forces
2. **Capability** - founder and team evolution, system redesign and strategic intervention
3. **Capital** - structured design deployed at the right time in the right way

When these three levers move together, transformation accelerates.
When any one lever is missing, friction appears and value

leaks.

Let's examine each.

1. Coherence - The Alignment That Compounds

Coherence is the first lever because incoherence is the silent killer of ventures.

Incoherence appears as:

- a strong product with a weak culture
- a brilliant founder with poor systems
- rapid top line growth with collapsing margins
- strong validation with poor structure
- clear mission with no capital strategy
- a team with passion but no narrative cohesion

Most companies do not fail because of one fatal flaw.

They fail from **the accumulation of small misalignments**.

Coherence is what happens when:

- structure matches strategy
- culture supports behaviour

- incentives match mission
- systems match scale
- capital supports timing
- people align around purpose
- impact aligns with growth
- and all forces reinforce each other

This is where the Compass becomes the engine.

By mapping the eight forces and revealing the Gap and X Factor, the Compass turns unknowns into knowns, chaos into pattern and pattern into design.

The moment a company is coherent, velocity appears.
Decisions become clearer.
Risk reduces.
Time compresses.
Growth accelerates.

Coherence is the amplifier of everything.

2. Capability - The Engine of Transformation

Capability is the second lever because capital without capability just accelerates dysfunction.

Companies fail from:

- leadership blind spots
- culture erosion
- poor sequencing
- strategic fog
- emotional immaturity
- lack of operational depth
- brittle governance
- unclear roles
- unintegrated teams

Capability is where the Ambassadors become central. The MAD ecosystem brings more than money. It brings:

- founders with scars and wisdom
- operators with pattern recognition
- educators with frameworks
- strategists with clarity
- technologists with experience
- cultural leaders with relational intelligence
- advisors with governance depth
- connectors with networks

- storytellers with narrative skill

This ecosystem surrounds each company with **collective intelligence**.

The principle is simple:

"A founder should never face a problem someone in our ecosystem has already solved."

Capability closes the Gap faster than capital ever could.

Capability:

- compresses time
- reduces risk
- saves money
- accelerates learning
- strengthens resilience
- deepens culture
- improves execution
- refines strategy
- and supports founder wellbeing

Capable companies do not just scale.
They evolve.

3. Capital - The Catalyst, Not the Cure

Capital is the third lever because capital alone cannot create transformation.

But capital deployed at the right moment, in the right structure, with the right intention becomes catalytic.

MAD's capital architecture emphasises:

- timing
- fit
- structure
- flexibility
- alignment
- resilience
- early DPI
- long term upside
- and impact integration

Capital that aligns with the Compass:

- strengthens coherence
- supports capability
- closes the Gap
- reduces pressure

- increases optionality
- amplifies ROI
- and stabilises the journey

Capital is not the solution.

Capital is the accelerant.

MAD treats capital as a design element, not an outcome.

The Sequence of Transformation

One of the most overlooked concepts in venture building is **sequencing**.

Even a great plan fails if built in the wrong order.

MAD's method follows a repeated sequence:

1. Reveal the Pattern

Use the Compass to map the eight forces, the X Factor and the Gap.

2. Diagnose the Leverage Point

Identify the smallest intervention that creates the greatest structural improvement.

3. Stabilise the System

Strengthen culture, structure and governance.

4. Build Capability

Deploy Ambassadors and ecosystem expertise.

5. Align Capital Strategy

Structure capital to match growth rhythm and reduce risk.

6. Execute the Transformation

Work with founders on the highest leverage interventions.

7. Scale the Outcome

Grow cleanly, coherently and with reduced friction.

This sequence repeats in cycles, each time expanding the company's capacity to grow and evolve.

Transformation is not one event.

It is a rhythm.

Why Repeatability Matters

Repeatability is not just a benefit for investors.

It is a benefit for founders, ventures, and the planet.

Repeatability:

- reduces founder burnout
- reduces learning curve
- reduces capital waste
- reduces execution error
- increases clarity
- increases stability
- increases impact
- increases speed
- increases success odds
- increases investor confidence
- increases societal value creation

Repeatability makes the future legible.

The Possible Planet requires not just belief, but *method*.

A Story of Repeatability in Action

We once worked with a company that had strong revenue but chaotic internal systems. The founder was charismatic but exhausted. The product was excellent but the culture was eroding. Investors were nervous. Growth had stalled.

Using the Compass, we mapped the forces. The Gap revealed:

- weak Structure
- misaligned People
- fragile Culture
- narrow Market Forces
- and a strong X Factor at the centre

The leverage point was not capital.
It was capability and coherence.

Within six months:

- a new COO was hired
- cultural repair work began
- governance was redesigned
- the pricing model evolved
- narrative clarity returned
- confidence resurfaced
- growth resumed

Capital was deployed later, not sooner.
When deployed, it accelerated a coherent system, not a chaotic one.

Repeatability turned what could have been failure into

momentum.

Integrated Systems Make Results Predictable

In traditional venture:

- success is random
- failure is normal
- capital is scattered
- guidance is ad hoc
- outcomes depend on luck

In integrated venture:

- success is patterned
- failure becomes insight
- capital is intentional
- capability is embedded
- outcomes are designed

Integrated investing is not a new asset class.
It is a new operating system for venture creation.

This is why MAD does not chase unicorns.
We build companies that solve real problems and scale coherently.

Repeatability is the antidote to volatility.

The Difference Between Helping a Company and Transforming It

Many investors help companies.
MAD transforms them.

Helping is tactical.
Transforming is systemic.

Helping is reactive.
Transforming is proactive.

Helping fixes symptoms.
Transforming rewires the system.
MAD transforms companies because:

- we see the whole
- we understand patterns
- we intervene at leverage points
- we integrate philosophy with practice
- we honour meaning and metrics together
- we give founders capability, not just capital

- we use the entire ecosystem as an amplifier
- and we build ventures inside planetary logic

Transformation is not about working harder.
It is about working in alignment.

This is how outcomes become repeatable.

Why MAD's Model Is Built for the Next Twenty Years

The next twenty years will belong to companies that:

- solve planetary and human challenges
- integrate values with value creation
- build capabilities faster than competitors
- operate inside planetary boundaries
- attract culturally aligned talent
- deploy capital strategically
- adapt intuitively and quickly
- and grow through coherence, not chaos

MAD's integrated model is purpose built for this reality.

It is not theory.
It is systems engineering for the future of venture.

The Bridge Strengthens

Chapter by chapter, we have now assembled:

- vision
- diagnosis
- philosophy
- tools
- architecture
- and the method of repeatable transformation

The bridge is almost complete.

What remains are the *engines* that move people and capital across that bridge:
- Philanthropy as Amplifier
- Government as Co-investor
- The Ecosystem as Village
- The Market as Proving Ground
- The Founder as Hero
- The Capital Engine as Catalyst

These forces come together in the next chapters to show how integrated investing becomes a global movement.

CHAPTER 10
THE MULTIPLIERS

*How Philanthropy, Government
and Catalytic Capital Accelerate the Future*

The Law of Leverage in Human Progress

Every major leap forward in civilisation has come from leverage.

Not force.

Not scale.

Not volume.

Leverage.

Fire leveraged energy.

Language leveraged collaboration.

Writing leveraged memory.

Printing leveraged knowledge.

Electricity leveraged labour.

The Internet leveraged information.

In our time, the greatest leverage point is not a technology.
It is not a policy.
It is not a market.

It is **capital architecture**.

When capital is deployed in isolation, change is incremental.
When capital is deployed in integrated layers, change becomes exponential.

This chapter is about those layers - the multipliers that turn good ideas into global solutions.

Why Most Capital Moves Too Slowly

Today, we face global challenges that do not wait for bureaucratic funding cycles or decade-long investment returns.
Climate instability, food insecurity, health inequity and ecological collapse operate on compounding curves.

But capital, as currently structured, often moves on linear timelines.

Philanthropy moves slowly because it is conservative and

bureaucratic.

Governments move slowly because they are risk averse and political.

Institutional finance moves slowly because it is governed by regulation and legacy mandates.

Venture capital moves quickly, but only toward narrow bands of opportunity.

The result:

- trillions of dollars
- enormous goodwill
- massive institutional capability
- world class innovators

all trapped inside **structural misalignment**.

To accelerate the transition to the Possible Planet, we must align these forces, not segregate them.

That alignment begins with catalytic capital.

Catalytic Capital, The First Domino

Catalytic capital is the form of capital that moves first.
It is the capital that absorbs risk others will not.

It signals confidence in the unknown and de-risks possibility for everyone else.

This is why catalytic capital is the **first domino** in systems change.

A single act of catalytic investment can:

- unlock private capital
- attract government co funding
- mobilise philanthropic networks
- compress deployment timelines
- validate emerging ventures
- and accelerate adoption of new technologies

It is not the size of catalytic capital that matters.
It is the timing.
Catalytic capital operates like ignition in an engine: small in absolute terms, but essential to spark motion.

MAD's architecture is built on this principle.

Philanthropy as Amplifier

Philanthropy holds trillions of dollars globally, yet only a small fraction is deployed into long term systemic solutions. Most sits idle in endowments invested conventionally, often counter to the missions they serve.

Philanthropy has been treated as charity.
It should be treated as leverage.

MAD's third founding principle (Chapter 8) reframed philanthropy as **first-loss catalytic capital**. A small philanthropic layer reduces perceived risk and increases investor confidence, often unlocking ten to twenty times more private and government capital.

When philanthropy becomes catalyst instead of subsidy:

- solutions scale faster
- risk is absorbed at the right layer
- early innovation becomes investable
- new markets become visible
- capital flows into essential sectors
- and the entire ecosystem accelerates

This is philanthropy not as donation, but as **economic ignition**.

Government as Co-Investor

Governments are not designed to take early risk.

The Multipliers

They are designed to institutionalise success once it is proven.

Catalytic capital creates the conditions governments need to participate.

When ventures reach a certain level of validation (commercial traction, capacity building, early impact), governments can:

- match investment
- subsidise cost reductions
- fund research
- enable infrastructure
- support regulation
- amplify reach
- create national programs
- and reduce systemic friction

This is the logic behind CEFC in Australia, InvestEU in Europe, ARPA H in the United States and catalytic sovereign programs across the Asia Pacific.

Governments are multipliers of proven models.
They turn early scale into societal scale.

But they rarely move first.

Catalytic capital pulls them into the equation.

Private Capital as the Engine

Once philanthropy de-risks and government institutionalises, private capital scales.

Private capital is:

- the engine of expansion
- the fuel of momentum
- the validator in markets
- the accelerator of adoption
- and the force that drives ventures into mainstream economics

When aligned with regenerative structures, private capital becomes the most powerful multiplier of all.

But private capital requires:

- clarity
- confidence
- de-risking
- structure
- timing
- and narrative

This is why the MAD Hyperscalers Fund is built on integrated principles rather than siloed ones.
It sits at the intersection, not on the sidelines.

The Multiplication Curve

When philanthropic, government and private capital are aligned, something extraordinary happens:
multiplication replaces addition.

Adding capital is linear.
Multiplying capital is exponential.

The multiplication curve looks like this:

Catalytic Philanthropy → Confident Private Capital → Government Co Funding → Market Adoption → System Transformation

One dollar of catalytic capital can produce ten or twenty dollars of private deployment and even more in government support.

Imagine:

- a $500k philanthropic layer unlocking $10m of private capital
- which triggers $15m of government co funding
- which generates $50m in downstream economic benefit
- which reduces carbon, restores ecosystems, or improves health outcomes
- which creates confidence in the next wave of innovators
- which accelerates the sector's entire growth curve

This is the leverage of integrated investing.

The "Village Effect" as a Multiplier

In Chapter 6, we explored the idea that it takes a village to raise a company.

The MAD ecosystem expands this idea.

The "village" is not only capability.
It is also a multiplier.

The collective intelligence of operators, founders, ambassadors, technologists, educators and advisors creates:

- faster decisions

- cleaner execution
- smarter sequencing
- better governance
- less waste
- fewer errors
- more resilience
- stronger culture
- deeper insight
- and accelerated growth

Capability multiplies capital.
Capital amplifies capability.
Together, they become a system.

This is why MAD's ecosystem is not an add on.
It is a central multiplier of ROI, impact and speed.

A Practical Example of Multipliers in Motion

Consider an early-scale agritech venture working on water conservation, one of the world's most urgent challenges.

Stage 1 - Catalytic Capital

A small philanthropic layer provides early deployment support, enabling the company to complete a pilot.

Stage 2 - Private Capital

MAD enters, structuring capital to support revenue expansion and operational stability.

Stage 3 - Government Activation

Proven savings in water usage make the venture eligible for government programs supporting drought resilience.

Stage 4 - Market Expansion

With government validation, industry adoption accelerates, and large enterprise customers join.

Stage 5 - System Transformation

Agricultural practices shift, resource usage declines and environmental resilience grows.

Multiplication Summary

A small catalytic spark triggers capital flows, system flows, policy flows and market flows, culminating in regenerative impact.

This pattern is repeatable.

Why Founders Need Multipliers

Most founders are asked to do the impossible:

- change systems
- build products
- create culture
- raise capital
- understand regulation
- manage teams
- define brand
- and maintain wellbeing

without leverage.

Multipliers give founders the advantage they need to enact system level change rather than incremental product change.

Multipliers turn ventures into movements.
Movements turn solutions into standards.
Standards turn innovations into normality.

Why Investors Need Multipliers

Investors often underestimate the degree to which external systems determine venture success.
The best return profile emerges when investors understand:

- how risk migrates,
- how capital layers interact,
- how policy amplifies,
- how culture accelerates,
- how capability reduces capital need,
- and how narrative shapes markets.

When investors understand multipliers, they stop chasing unicorns and start building systems.

This is regenerative ROI.

Why the World Needs Multipliers

The scale of global challenges - ecological collapse, democratic fragility, food insecurity, public health decline - requires leverage points, not incrementalism.

We cannot solve today's problems with yesterday's deployment mechanisms.

Multipliers create:

- speed
- alignment
- legitimacy

- coverage
- system pathways
- shared vision
- scalable outcomes

They turn the Possible Planet from theory into practice.

The Birth of Regenerative Capital Movements

There is a growing global movement toward regenerative capital.

You can feel it in:

- family offices shifting from ESG to system level visions,
- philanthropists seeking leverage rather than charity,
- governments funding climate transition,
- founders building mission tied models,
- investors prioritising coherence,
- communities demanding authenticity,
- and global institutions exploring blended finance.

MAD sits inside this emerging movement as both practitioner and proof point.

Multipliers make this movement real.
They give it teeth.

They give it speed.
They give it scale.

The Path Ahead

The first nine chapters of this book created the map:

- The Possible Planet
- The Current Reality
- The Crisis of Meaning
- The End of the Growth Paradigm
- The Origin of MAD
- The Compass
- Integration
- Capital Architecture
- Repeatable Outcomes

Chapter 10 expands the map into a **system for scaling transformation**.

Multipliers are how civilization moves from fragmentation to coherence.
They are how integrated investing moves from niche to norm.
They are how founders become system actors.
They are how investors become system architects.
They are how societies cross thresholds.

The next chapters explore how this becomes a movement - not just a fund, philosophy or model, but a cultural force capable of reshaping the 21st century.

CHAPTER 11
THE MOVEMENT OF MAD

When Capital Becomes Community

Every Transformation Begins With a Story

Civilisations do not change because of technology alone.
They change because of **stories** and the people bold enough to live them.

The green revolution began with a story about feeding a hungry world.
The civil rights movement began with a story about dignity.
The environmental movement began with a story about guardianship of the Earth.
The digital revolution began with a story about connection.

The regenerative revolution, the one we are now entering, begins with a story about **coherence**.
About reintegrating what has been separated.
About aligning capital with consequence, business with biosphere, profit with purpose, and innovation with humanity.

This is not a corporate initiative.
It is not a policy program.
It is a movement.

And MAD is one expression of that movement.

From Fund to Philosophy to Field

MAD began as a fund, then became a philosophy, then something larger, a living field of people, practices and partnerships that extend far beyond the boundaries of any capital vehicle.

This field includes:

- founders solving planetary problems,
- operators who have lived the journey,
- investors who see capital as stewardship,
- technologists building regenerative tools,
- cultural figures shaping narrative,
- educators reshaping learning,
- philanthropists acting as catalysts,
- and ambassadors committed to making a difference.

The MAD ecosystem is not a network in the transactional sense.

It is a **movement space** - a place where aligned individuals collaborate toward the Possible Planet.

It operates on a simple principle:

"A founder should never have to walk alone.
A venture should never be built in isolation.
And capital should never move without conscience."

Why Movements Matter More Than Models

A model can scale a company.
But a movement can scale a civilisation.

Movements:

- shift culture,
- normalize new behaviours,
- attract early adopters,
- nurture community,
- generate shared identity,
- accelerate learning cycles,
- and transform abstract ideas into lived norms.

Movements spread not through contracts,
but through **conviction**.

Impact investing created a model.
Integrated investing creates a movement.

MAD is one node of that movement,
but the movement is far bigger than MAD.

Founders as System Healers

In every movement, there are protagonists - individuals who embody the transition, who hold both the wounds and the potential of the world they are trying to change.

Founders are these protagonists.

Founders are society's frontline.
They respond to what is broken by building what is missing.
They sense the future before the present catches up.
They hold the tension between what is and what could be.
But founders do more than innovate.
They heal.

They heal:

- broken supply chains,
- broken food systems,
- broken energy systems,
- broken education systems,
- broken health systems,
- broken ecological cycles.

And sometimes, founders heal themselves in the process - stepping into purpose, overcoming fear, maturing into leaders who shape culture from the inside out.

The MAD ecosystem exists to support founders in this deeper role.
Not only as CEOs, but as **system healers**.

Investors as Stewards of Possibility

Traditional investors see themselves as allocators.
Integrated investors see themselves as stewards.

Stewardship means:

- understanding the systems a venture touches,
- respecting the long term,
- investing in capability as much as capital,
- supporting founders' development,
- keeping companies within planetary boundaries,
- amplifying community and culture,
- and embedding purpose at the heart of decision making.

Investors are not outside the story.
They are inside it.

Every investor becomes part of the movement narrative.
Every dollar carries intention into the world.
Every investment is an act of authorship.

When investors act as stewards, they transform not only companies but ecosystems.

The Role of the Ambassadors

The MAD Ambassador group is the heartbeat of the movement.

These are not advisers in the transactional sense.
They are **elders** in the entrepreneurial-adjacent world.
They carry the scars of lived experience, the wisdom of patterns, and the humility that only comes from building, failing, and building again.

Ambassadors are:

- operators,
- founders,
- technologists,

- strategists,
- storytellers,
- activists,
- connectors,
- and thinkers.

Their presence multiplies the intelligence of the ecosystem.

Ambassadors:

- reduce founder loneliness,
- increase resilience,
- expand networks,
- accelerate culture change,
- strengthen leadership,
- clarify strategy,
- and reopen possibility when founders hit walls.

This is not mentoring.
This is **collective stewardship**.
The Ambassadors turn the Compass from a diagnostic tool into a lived practice,
and the Gap from a challenge into a journey.

The Village Model of Venture

We said earlier that it takes a village to raise a child.
It also takes a village to raise a company.

This is not metaphorical. It is structural.

The world's most successful ecosystems - Silicon Valley, Tel Aviv, Shenzhen, Bangalore - all thrived because of community density, shared norms, knowledge exchange, relational trust and cultural coherence.

MAD intentionally creates these conditions for purpose-driven ventures.

The Village Model means:

- founders do not solve problems alone,
- leadership is developed intentionally,
- culture is supported consciously,
- capital is deployed wisely,
- risk is shared intelligently,
- and successes are celebrated collectively.

This is not venture as competition.
It is venture as community.

Community produces velocity.

Velocity produces outcomes.
Outcomes attract movement.
Movement scales impact.
Impact builds new systems.

Narrative as Infrastructure

Every movement needs a story strong enough to hold it together.

The story of MAD is not "an investment fund."

It is:

"Capital as a force for regeneration."

"Companies as instruments of healing."

"Investors as stewards of possibility."

"The village as the multiplier."

"The Possible Planet as the horizon."

Story is not decoration.

Story is infrastructure.

Narrative:

- gives coherence to complexity,
- provides emotional energy,

- clarifies identity,
- invites collaboration,
- and attracts aligned people.

Founders need narrative.

Investors need narrative.

Movements require narrative.

MAD's narrative is the connective tissue that binds integrated capital, founder development, ecological reality and cultural meaning into one living whole.

Movements Spread Through People, Not Through Products

A movement spreads when:

- people see themselves in it,
- they feel part of something larger,
- they recognise their gifts are needed,
- they are energised by belonging,
- and they believe in the story.

MAD's movement grows not by marketing,

but by resonance.

A founder tells another founder.
An Ambassador encourages a colleague.
An investor shares the philosophy with a family member.
A policymaker sees alignment.
A community benefits from a venture's work.
A student is inspired by a narrative of possibility.

Movements grow by relationship.
They scale by trust.
They deepen by coherence.

The Global Convergence

Around the world, parallel movements are emerging:

- regenerative agriculture,
- circular economy,
- clean energy transition,
- indigenous knowledge integration,
- inner development goals,
- conscious capitalism,
- philanthropic catalysis,
- blended finance innovation,
- youth climate mobilisation,

- mission driven technology,
- systems leadership networks.

MAD is one expression of a deeper global shift.
A shift from extraction to regeneration.
From fragmentation to integration.
From ego to ecosystem.
From competition to collaboration.
From capital as force to capital as stewardship.

The movement is not coming.
It has arrived.

MAD is simply one of the early storytellers, architects and practitioners.

A Personal Moment: When the Movement Became Visible

There was a moment when we saw the movement as more than theory.

It was not at a boardroom table or an investor meeting.
It was at a gathering with founders, operators, Ambassadors, investors and community partners — all speaking from different industries, different generations, different skill sets.

What struck me was not the diversity.
It was the coherence.

Everyone was speaking the same underlying language:

- purpose,
- regeneration,
- stewardship,
- possibility,
- systems,
- courage,
- meaning,
- resilience.

In that moment, I realised MAD was not simply building ventures.
It was participating in a cultural evolution.
A shift in consciousness.
A movement.

We were no longer building companies.
We were building coherence.

Where the Movement Leads Next

Chapter 11 marks a transition.
We have explored:

- the vision,
- the crises,
- the philosophy,
- the architecture,
- the tools,
- the repeatable method,
- and now the movement.

What comes next is **the human future of this movement** - the people who carry it forward, the relational depth that sustains it and the integrated pathways that will define the next chapter of human potential.

The next chapter explores the heart of this:
Capital of the Heart - the inner dimension of leadership, purpose and stewardship that makes integrated investing not just effective, but transformative.

CHAPTER 12
CAPITAL OF THE HEART

*The Inner Dimension of Leadership,
Stewardship and Human Potential*

The Most Important Capital Is Not on the Balance Sheet

For all our technology and metrics, for all our dashboards and diagnostics, for all our systems and frameworks, civilisation still turns on something older and deeper:

the human heart.

Not the sentimental heart,
not the fragile heart,
but the courageous heart that chooses purpose over fear,
integrity over convenience,
alignment over approval,
and stewardship over extraction.

The Possible Planet will not be built only by capital strategy, innovation or policy.
It will be built by the **inner evolution of the people** who deploy those tools.

Capital of the Heart is not a metaphor.
It is a missing economic variable.

When leaders develop internally, systems change externally.
The Inner Landscape Shapes the Outer World
Every founder carries within them:

- their history,
- their wounds,
- their ambitions,
- their fears,
- their intuition,
- their patterns,
- their gifts,
- and the worldview through which they interpret reality.

Every investor carries the same.

These inner landscapes shape decisions more than data ever will.

They determine:

- how founders respond to pressure,
- whether investors act from courage or caution,
- whether a board chooses cooperation or control,
- whether a team grows together or fractures apart,
- whether a company chooses short term wins or long term integrity.

The interior world is not separate from the economy.
It is the economy's operating system.

As the saying goes:

"We don't see the world as it is.
We see the world as we are."

Capital of the Heart recognises that integrated investing is not merely a structural model.
It is a **human development model**.

Leadership as a Journey of Consciousness

Leadership is not a job description.
Leadership is a developmental stage.

Some leaders operate from survival.
Some from ambition.
Some from achievement.
Some from service.
Some from stewardship.

The difference is not intelligence - it is **consciousness**.

Integrated companies require integrated leaders - leaders who can:

- hold paradox
- sense what is emerging
- regulate emotion
- make principled decisions
- communicate with clarity
- face uncertainty without collapse
- align teams through purpose
- choose long horizons over short wins
- and act from integrity rather than impulse

These are not soft skills.
They are civilisation-building skills.

They determine everything from founder wellbeing to cultural resilience, governance quality, talent retention and strategic clarity.

The Emotional Infrastructure of Founders

Every founder carries a psychological structure that either amplifies or constrains their potential.

Founders who scale well often have:

- high self awareness
- emotional literacy
- mature conflict capacity
- the ability to receive feedback
- a strong sense of purpose
- resilience and adaptability
- healthy boundaries
- intuitive intelligence
- the ability to metabolise failure
- and relational trust

Founders who struggle often battle:

- perfectionism
- people pleasing
- scarcity mindsets
- unresolved trauma

- avoidance of conflict
- imposter syndrome
- obsession with control
- hyper achievement patterns
- and fear of disappointing investors

A founder's inner architecture becomes the company's outer architecture.

The Compass reveals the organizational pattern.
Capital of the Heart reveals the human pattern.

Successful integrated investing requires both.

Investors as Carriers of Energy

Just as founders shape companies, investors shape founders.

When investors operate from fear, founders absorb that fear.
When investors demand hypergrowth, founders distort their mission.
When investors project anxiety, teams destabilise.
When investors model scarcity, companies shrink their vision.
When investors model courage, founders expand.

Investors carry emotional energy into every room.
That energy either restricts or expands possibility.

Investors who embody stewardship behave differently. They:

- listen more than they speak
- ask deeper questions
- understand timing
- respect complexity
- prioritise coherence
- encourage founder wellbeing
- value meaning as much as metrics
- make decisions with moral clarity
- and lean into courage rather than safety

Investors who lead from the heart create companies that lead from the heart.

This is not idealism.
This is leadership physics.

The Role of Inner Development in Systems Change

The Inner Development Goals (IDGs), an emerging global framework complementary to the UN's Sustainable Development Goals, identify five dimensions essential for modern leadership:

1. **Being** - inner anchoring, presence, self awareness
2. **Thinking** - critical reflection, holistic analysis, complexity understanding
3. **Relating** - empathy, connection, communication
4. **Collaborating** – co-creation, trust building, conflict resolution
5. **Acting** - courage, agency, long termism, resilience

These inner capacities mirror exactly what founders and investors in regenerative industries require.

Integrated investing is not simply a capital strategy.
It is the embodiment of the IDGs.

The Possible Planet requires:

- emotional maturity,
- systemic depth,
- relational wisdom,
- courage under uncertainty,
- humility in the face of complexity,
- and the willingness to grow internally to meet external challenges.

Systems cannot transform faster than the people who run them.

The Long Arc of Human Potential

Every founder, investor and team member is on a developmental journey.

Their growth is not only personal but strategic.

When leaders move to deeper developmental stages:

- decisions simplify
- clarity increases
- ego softens
- purpose strengthens
- intuition sharpens
- presence deepens
- and culture stabilises

This has direct economic consequences:

- better governance
- lower burn rates
- higher retention
- cleaner strategy

- lower conflict costs
- reduced chaos
- higher execution quality
- faster scaling
- longer term alignment
- and superior ROI

Human evolution becomes business evolution.

The most valuable resource in the 21st century is not data. It is consciousness.

A Personal Reflection: The Founder Who Became a Leader

I once worked with a founder who was brilliant, driven and visionary, but overwhelmed.
The company was growing quickly, but culture was fracturing.
He was trapped in firefighting mode, exhausted and reactive.

During one conversation, he said quietly,
"I know what the company needs. I just don't know how to become the person it needs me to be."

That sentence was the turning point.

Over the next year, he:

- learned to regulate his stress
- built a leadership team he trusted
- delegated without fear
- clarified his purpose
- deepened communication
- stabilised culture
- redesigned structure
- and reconnected with the meaning that brought him to the work

The company doubled in size.
Conflict decreased.
Retention increased.
Margins expanded.
Investors regained confidence.

Nothing changed until **he** changed.

Capital of the Heart is the leverage point of leaders.

Why Culture Begins in the Heart

Culture is not created through slogans, posters or HR

documents.

It emerges from the emotional tone of leadership.

Leaders model:

- honesty,
- curiosity,
- openness,
- courage,
- humility,
- trust,
- and repair.

Teams imitate what leaders embody.

Culture emanates from the interior world of the founder.

Values are not declared. They are demonstrated.

A leader who acts from the heart creates psychological safety.

Psychological safety creates innovation.

Innovation creates resilience.

Resilience creates scale.

Scale creates impact.

This is the compounding effect of integrity.

Capital of the Heart in the MAD Ecosystem

MAD's emphasis on purpose, coherence and stewardship is not cosmetic. It is systemic.

MAD Ambassadors do not simply bring skill. They bring:

- emotional intelligence
- relational wisdom
- depth of experience
- calmness under pressure
- pattern recognition
- and grounded presence

Founders are not machines.
They are humans carrying enormous weight.

They need a village not just for capability, but for **belonging**.

MAD's community provides:
- emotional support
- narrative clarity
- leadership development

- perspective in crisis
- truth without judgment
- strength without dominance
- and companionship in complexity

Capital of the Heart is not a supplement to the MAD model. It is one of its pillars.

Why the Future of Capital Is Interior

The transition from extraction to regeneration,

from fragmentation to integration,

from competition to coherence,

from fear to stewardship,

will require an internal shift equal to the external one.

AI cannot provide this shift.

Technology cannot automate it.

Markets cannot price it.

Policy cannot legislate it.

It comes from the human beings inside the system.

It comes from their courage, empathy, presence, maturity and clarity.

It comes from the heart.

We do not build the Possible Planet only with capital design. We build it with **human design**.

The future will belong to leaders who evolve inwardly as they create outwardly.

This is not optional.
It is structural.

The Strength of Soft Power

In the 20th century, power was measured in industrial capacity, GDP, military might and market share.

In the 21st century, power is shifting toward:

- relational trust
- emotional intelligence
- meaning-making
- intuition
- narrative clarity
- systems thinking
- moral courage
- psychological safety
- and the ability to mobilise human potential

Soft power is not soft.
It is subtle power.
It is the power that shapes worlds quietly.

MAD's approach combines hard power (capital, structure, strategy)
and soft power (heart, meaning, connection)
into a single integrated approach.

This is the new leadership.

The Heart as the Final Multiplier

We often think of multipliers as external forces - catalytic capital, government co funding, policy shifts. But the greatest multiplier of all is internal.

A founder with a coherent heart is unstoppable.
A team with a coherent culture is unshakeable.
An investor with a coherent purpose is uncorruptible.
A movement with a coherent vision is inevitable.

The heart is the amplifier of all other amplifiers.

It is the place where courage replaces fear,
where clarity replaces confusion,

and where meaning replaces exhaustion.

Capital of the Heart turns leaders into stewards,
companies into communities,
and movements into transformations.

Where the Heart Leads Next

Chapter 12 closes the inner dimension of integration.
We have now explored:

- the map,
- the philosophy,
- the architecture,
- the movement,
- and the heart.

What comes next is the **Return** - the outward expansion,
the tangible case studies,
the systemic outcomes,
and the convergence of everything into a vision of the world that is possible.

Chapter 13 turns from interior transformation to external demonstration:

The Possible Planet - The Future We Could Build.

MAD - What the World Needs Now Is a Little Madness

CHAPTER 13
THE POSSIBLE PLANET

The Future We Could Build

We Return to the Vision, But With New Eyes

Back in the Prologue, we imagined a world that felt almost utopian at first glance — abundant clean energy, restored ecosystems, thriving communities, coherent economies, purposeful work and an integration between human systems and natural systems that felt as poetic as it did plausible.

Now, after twelve chapters of philosophy, structure and transformation,
the Possible Planet no longer feels idealistic.
It feels inevitable - if we have the courage to design it.

This chapter is the return to that horizon.
The place where everything we have learned converges into a future that is not fantasy, but blueprint.

Every civilisation carries within it a latent future, one waiting to be built.

The Possible Planet is the future latent within ours.

A World Aligned with Itself

Imagine a civilisation in which the major systems of life are finally aligned:

- food systems designed for nourishment and regeneration, not scale for scale's sake
- energy systems designed for abundance, not depletion
- education designed for lifelong learning, not standardised sorting
- healthcare designed for wellbeing, not treatment
- technology designed for augmentation, not exploitation
- governance designed for participation, not polarisation
- capital designed for regeneration, not extraction

A civilisation where coherence is the organising principle.

Where the inner world of people and the outer world of systems harmonise rather than collide.

This is not utopia.

This is the Possible Planet.

It is a world where:

- ecosystems recover faster than they degrade,
- communities rise faster than they fracture,
- innovation reduces fragility rather than amplifying it,
- and business becomes an instrument of healing rather than harm.

The Possible Planet Begins with Energy

Every civilisation is defined by how it generates and uses energy.

Humanity's first energy transition came from fire.
Its second came from fossil fuels.
Its third will come from **abundant, clean, decentralised and increasingly autonomous energy systems.**

On the Possible Planet:

- solar and wind are the backbone,
- storage systems provide continuous stability,

- geothermal and tidal supplement with reliability,
- fusion moves from theory to infrastructure,
- and microgrids give communities energy sovereignty.

Energy becomes **too cheap to meter**.
This single shift unlocks:

- water desalination at scale
- vertical farming in cities
- low cost manufacturing
- reduced geopolitical conflict
- global cold chains for food security
- and entire new industries built on abundance instead of scarcity

Clean energy is not only an environmental solution.
It is the foundation upon which regeneration becomes physically possible.

Capital designed for coherence accelerates this.

Food Systems That Nourish and Restore

The future of food is decentralised, regenerative and technologically augmented.
On the Possible Planet:

- soil is alive, not depleted
- farms are data-rich ecosystems
- precision fermentation supplements nutrition
- seaweed farms rebuild oceans
- supply chains become transparent
- waste becomes input
- nutrient cycles close
- and food security becomes a global right, not a regional privilege

Agriculture shifts from extraction to partnership with nature.

Capital flows into ventures like:
- regenerative land management
- water-efficient production
- carbon-positive farming
- nutrient mapping
- and climate resistant crops

This is not just sustainability.
It is systemic renewal.

Health Systems That Heal, Not Manage Decline

The Possible Planet treats health as a continuum, not a

reaction.

- diagnostics become continuous and personalised
- mental health is integrated into primary care
- digital therapeutics augment human practitioners
- prevention becomes more profitable than treatment
- healthcare systems move from reactive to anticipatory
- addiction recovery is evidence based and stigma free
- and the global south is not an afterthought, but a centre of innovation

Capital that flows into regenerative health models reduces global burden of disease more efficiently than any government policy alone.

Integrated investing aligns:

- physiology and psychology,
- technology and humanity,
- longevity and wellbeing.

The result is a healthier civilisation in every sense of the word.

Education for a World That Changes Fast

The Possible Planet's education systems mirror the

complexity and speed of the real world.

- AI tutors support every learner individually
- experiential learning replaces passive consumption
- creativity and systems thinking become core subjects
- vocational pathways are fluid and lifelong
- intergenerational learning strengthens communities
- and education reconnects people to meaning, not just employment

Education becomes less about memorisation and more about transformation.

Founders who understand purpose and coherence become role models, not exceptions.

Technology as a Partner in Human Evolution

The Possible Planet is not anti-technology.
It is pro wisdom.

Technology becomes:

- partner, not master
- amplifier, not replacement
- augmentation, not domination

Artificial intelligence:

- reduces drudgery
- protects against cognitive overload
- improves safety in dangerous industries
- accelerates scientific discovery
- and deepens rather than diminishes human capability

The Possible Planet uses technology to expand humanity, not compress it.

Culture as the Invisible Infrastructure

A civilisation is healthy when its culture supports:

- belonging
- creativity
- compassion
- pluralism
- curiosity
- and courage

The Possible Planet values art as much as science,
community as much as productivity,
ritual as much as innovation.

Cultural health becomes a metric, not an afterthought.

Integrated capital recognises that culture is not soft, it is **structural**.

Governance That Reflects Complexity

Governance in the Possible Planet evolves from industrial era hierarchy into networked leadership that:

- listens
- decentralises
- protects
- learns
- iterates
- collaborates
- adapts

Democracy becomes participatory.
Policy becomes predictive.
Regulation becomes adaptive.

Public leadership becomes regenerative.

Government becomes a multiplier, not an inhibitor.

Capital, Reimagined

In the Possible Planet, capital behaves differently:

- it flows into essential sectors
- it rewards stewardship
- it amplifies community resilience
- it supports human development
- it regenerates ecological systems
- it integrates social and cultural dimensions
- it builds capability, not dependency
- it honours time
- it internalises externalities
- it values coherence over extraction

This is the world that emerges when capital is structured intentionally.

MAD is one architect of this shift,
but the movement is larger than any one system.

Integrated investing is the operating system of the Possible Planet.

What Becomes Possible When We Align

When energy becomes abundant,
food becomes secure,

health becomes proactive,
education becomes lifelong,
culture becomes coherent,
technology becomes humane,
governance becomes adaptive,
people become empowered,
and capital becomes regenerative...

Civilisation moves into its next evolutionary phase.

Human potential expands.
Ecological systems recover.
Political conflict reduces.
Inequality declines.
Innovation accelerates.
Communities flourish.
Fear recedes.
Creativity rises.
Wisdom returns.

The Possible Planet is not a fantasy.
It is the result of coherent design.

A Personal Reflection: Seeing the Future in the Present

There have been moments, working with founders and Ambassadors, when I have caught glimpses of the Possible Planet already alive in the present.

Moments where a founder describes a breakthrough that will change agriculture.
Moments where a team rebuilds a broken culture with honesty and courage.
Moments where investors choose purpose over fear.
Moments where government and private capital collaborate for genuine outcomes.
Moments where a community rallies around a venture that matters.
Moments where you sense the emergence of coherence.

These moments are small on the surface,
but they are seismic beneath.
They are the seeds of the civilisation we could build.

The Possible Planet is already here,
in pockets, in prototypes, in people.
It simply needs scale.

Why the Possible Planet Matters Now

We stand at a turning point in human history.

The next twenty years will determine:

- the livability of the planet,
- the legitimacy of democracy,
- the resilience of food systems,
- the future of work,
- the ethical shape of AI,
- global population health,
- and the trajectory of civilisation.

If we continue with the old story,
we threaten everything.
If we choose the new story,
we renew everything.

The Possible Planet is not just about what we build.
It is about who we become as we build it.

The Return, Now Complete

In every Hero's Journey, the protagonist returns home with the elixir - the knowledge or gift that transforms the village.

In the collective story of humanity, the "elixir" is integrated investing: the design of capital, culture, capability and consciousness into one coherent system.

We began this book with a vision.
We return to it now with structure, clarity, evidence and belief.

The Possible Planet is achievable.
But it requires:

- courage,
- coherence,
- community,
- capability,
- conscious capital,
- and the willingness to be a little MAD.

Where We Go From Here

The next chapter draws these strands together by bringing us home to the emotional and philosophical heart of this book - **The Beautiful Madness of Belief.**

This is where the Possible Planet becomes not only vision and design, but invitation.

PART III
THE RETURN

CHAPTER 14
THE BEAUTIFUL MADNESS OF BELIEF

The Courage to Build What the World Needs Next

The Hero Returns With the Elixir

Every great story follows an ancient arc.
The protagonist leaves the familiar world,
faces trials in the wilderness,
descends into the inner cave,
discovers the hidden truth,
and returns to their community transformed.

They return not just wiser,
but carrying something the community needs -
a gift, an insight, an elixir.

This book has followed that arc, not only for ventures or founders,
but for capital itself and for civilisation at large.

We left the world as it is.

We journeyed through the world as it could be.

We confronted the world as it has become.

We traced the bridge between despair and design.

We engineered a new story for capital.

We demonstrated proof in practice.

And now we return with the elixir -

the integrated worldview that makes transformation possible.

What we return with is not a fund,

but a belief.

A kind of beautiful madness.

The World Needs Belief Before It Needs Capital

We live in a moment of extraordinary possibility and extraordinary fear.

Never before have we had so much capability,

and never before have we had so much uncertainty.

People do not lack information.

They lack orientation.

They lack belief that change is possible.

They lack a story that can contain both the darkness of the present

and the potential of the future.

Capital alone cannot solve this.
Technology alone cannot solve this.
Policy alone cannot solve this.

Belief is the missing ingredient.

Not blind optimism,
but grounded, integrated belief -
the belief that humanity still has time,
still has wisdom,
still has imagination,
still has courage,
still has the capacity to evolve.

Belief that we can build something better than what we inherited.

Belief that we can heal the systems we have broken.
Belief that we can rise to meet the challenges of our age.

Belief that the Possible Planet is not a dream
but a design choice.

The Madness of Imagining Something Better

MAD - What the World Needs Now Is a Little Madness

It is easy to accept the world as it is.
It is safe to comply.
It is efficient to follow the patterns already laid out by others.
It is rational to conclude that we are too late,
too divided,
too exhausted,
too entangled in the old system to build something new.

But history has never belonged to the rational.
It has belonged to the unreasonable,
the visionaries,
the inventors,
the misfits,
the stewards,
the builders,
the ones willing to be called "mad"
for imagining something better.

The Possible Planet requires this kind of madness -
the madness of believing in coherence
in an incoherent world.

This madness is beautiful because it is necessary.
It is the antidote to apathy.
It is the spark of every innovation,
every movement,

every renaissance humanity has ever known.

MAD exists to model this.

To show that madness, when disciplined,

when integrated,

when aligned with systems thinking and purpose,

becomes the most powerful force of progress in the world.

Madness and Method

If this book has shown anything, it is that belief without structure collapses,

and structure without belief calcifies.

We need both.

The madness to dream boldly,

and the method to execute precisely.

MAD represents the fusion of these two energies.

Vision + Architecture.
Intuition + Analysis.
Meaning + Metrics.
Capital + Capability.
Courage + Coherence.

The madness gives us the Why.

The method gives us the How.

This duality is the essence of integrated investing.

The Courage to Care

Underneath everything in this book lies a deeper truth:
that caring is not naive,
not weak,
not sentimental
but courageous.

Care is the most underrated form of intelligence.

It fuels persistence.
It sharpens intuition.
It strengthens culture.
It clarifies decisions.
It attracts talent.
It legitimises capital.
It stabilises leadership.
It sustains movements.

Care is the hidden engine of regeneration.

The future will be built by the people who care enough

to challenge extraction,

to redesign systems,

to heal what is broken,

to steward what is vulnerable,

and to imagine a world worthy of the next generation.

Care is not an emotion.

Care is a strategy.

And one day soon, it will also be an asset class.

The Responsibility of Wealth

Those who control capital today carry a responsibility far larger than return profiles.

They carry responsibility for the direction of civilisation.

This is not hyperbole.

It is simple mechanics.

Capital funds:

- the technologies we use,
- the cities we live in,
- the education we receive,
- the foods we eat,
- the medicines we rely on,
- the work we perform,
- and the ecosystems we depend on.

Capital does not just influence the world.
It authors it.

The next chapter of civilisation will be written by investors who understand this responsibility and act accordingly.

Stewardship is the new sophistication.

The Responsibility of Founders

Founders are the healers, the innovators and the translators between the world that exists and the world that could exist.

Their responsibility is profound.

They must:

- hold vision and execution
- navigate complexity and uncertainty
- build culture while building product
- lead people while evolving personally
- stay connected to purpose while facing pressure
- remain human while carrying enormous weight

Founders are on their own hero's journey.

They need community,
guidance,
wisdom,
capital fit for purpose,
and ecosystems that reduce the loneliness of leadership.

The founders who succeed in the next era will not be the ones who move fastest.
They will be the ones who move **coherently**.

The Responsibility of Communities

Community is not peripheral.
It is central.

No company scales without community.
No movement grows without community.
No civilisation thrives without community.

Communities:

- create norms,
- enforce accountability,
- protect values,
- share knowledge,
- transmit culture,

- and build belonging.

Belonging is not a soft concept.
It is a productivity multiplier.
It is a mental health stabiliser.
It is a resilience generator.
It is a cultural foundation.

The Possible Planet will be built by communities of meaning, not individuals of ambition.

The Responsibility of Ourselves

Integrated investing is not merely an external transformation.
It is an internal one.

It asks us to develop the inner capacities required for the world we are trying to build:

- patience,
- humility,
- wisdom,
- courage,
- empathy,
- presence,
- self awareness,

- integrity,
- curiosity,
- and resilience.

If we want a regenerative world,
we must become regenerative people.

The systems we design reflect the consciousness we bring to them.

This is the deepest truth of the Possible Planet:
that the outer world is the shadow of the inner one.

The Path Ahead

We will not build the Possible Planet overnight.
But we can build it in increments,
in projects,
in ventures,
in ecosystems,
in partnerships,
in policy,
in culture,
and in ourselves.

We can build it by:

- funding the ventures that matter,
- supporting the founders who heal,
- designing the capital that regenerates,
- strengthening the communities that sustain,
- aligning government and philanthropy,
- amplifying the stories that inspire,
- and evolving the leaders who guide.

This is not simple.
It is not easy.
But it is possible.

Every civilisation chooses the stories that define it.
We are choosing ours right now.

The Invitation

So here, at the end of this book,
is the invitation:

Be MAD.
Be willing to imagine boldly.
Be willing to act courageously.
Be willing to feel deeply.
Be willing to design intentionally.

Be willing to challenge the old story.
Be willing to participate in the new one.
Be willing to invest in coherence.
Be willing to steward capital with conscience.
Be willing to join the movement of regeneration.

The world does not need more cynics.
It does not need more spectators.
It does not need more bystanders.

The world needs people willing to be a little mad -
not irrational,
but courageous,
not reckless,
but visionary,
not chaotic,
but coherent.

The sanity of our future depends on the beautiful madness of those who choose to make a difference.

This Is the Moment

We are alive at the turning point of history.
The decisions we make in this decade will define centuries.

We can build a world of breakdown or breakthrough.

We can choose extraction or regeneration.

We can choose fear or imagination.

We can choose fragmentation or integration.

The Possible Planet is ready.

The movement is growing.

The tools are here.

The capital is abundant.

The founders are rising.

The systems are shifting.

And the future is inviting us forward.

All it asks is one thing:

that we dare to believe.

THE BEAUTIFUL MADNESS OF BELIEF

Let this be the closing line,
the pulse beneath the book,
the whisper of every chapter:

Impact was the message.
Integration is the method.
MAD is the movement.
The Possible Planet is the destination.
And belief is the bridge.

EPILOGUE
PROOF IN PRACTICE

A Living Library of Case Studies

The Possible Planet is not built in theory.

It is built in companies, communities and movements all across the world - founders who choose purpose, investors who choose stewardship, and ecosystems that choose coherence over extraction.

Throughout this book, we have explored the philosophy, frameworks and architecture that make this transformation possible. But the most powerful demonstrations of integrated investing are always the real projects, ventures and leaders building the future today.

Rather than freeze this book in time with a fixed list of examples, we want the proof to remain **alive**, **current**, and **constantly renewing**.

The world changes fast.

Case studies evolve.

New pioneers emerge.

Innovations accelerate.

Impact deepens.

And the movement grows.

So instead of anchoring this book to examples destined to age, we are inviting you into a **living library** - a digital space that evolves as the movement evolves.

This page contains:

- up-to-date case studies of MAD-supported ventures,
- global examples of regenerative companies,
- integrated investing in action,
- system-level transformations across energy, food, health and culture,
- and curated profiles of founders, investors and communities building the Possible Planet.

It is updated regularly and reflects *the world as it is becoming.*

Visit: www.mad.vc/possibleplanet

There, you will find the stories, ventures and models that show the Possible Planet emerging in real time.
Some are born inside MAD's ecosystem.
Many come from the broader global movement.
All demonstrate the same truth:

Coherence scales.
Purpose transforms.
Integrated investing works.
And the Possible Planet is already underway.

This book ends here,
but the evidence is alive and ongoing.
The movement continues.
The story continues.
And now,
you are part of it.

ABOUT THE AUTHOR

Mark Falzon is an entrepreneur, investor and author with more than forty-five years of experience building, scaling and advising ventures across Australia, Asia and the United States. He is the co-founder of MAD Ventures and the Venture Compass and the creator of the Métis frameworks, and he is a leading voice in the emerging field of integrated investing.

Mark's work spans food security, environmental resilience, clean energy, health systems innovation, regenerative capital design and leadership development. His approach blends systems thinking, philosophical depth and operator wisdom to help founders and investors build ventures that make a meaningful difference in the world.

A lifelong student of human potential, Mark brings a unique combination of strategic clarity, emotional intelligence and mythic imagination to his work. He believes the next era of capitalism must be anchored in purpose, coherence and courage, and that the world needs not just better ideas, but better stories and better systems.

Mark lives in NSW Australia, where he continues to mentor founders, advise family offices, design regenerative capital structures and steward the growing movement behind MAD.

www.ingramcontent.com/pod-product-compliance
Lightning Source LLC
Chambersburg PA
CBHW050859160426
43194CB00011B/2222